COVID-19 and the Indian Economy

Impact and Response

COVID-19 and the Indian Economy

Impact and Response

Niranjan Sahoo
Professor of Disaster Management,
Xavier Institute of Social Service (XISS), Ranchi;
Advisor, National Productivity Council,
Ministry of Industry and Commerce,
Government of India

and

Mukunda Chandra Sahoo
Associate Professor,
Department of Hospital Administration,
All India Institute of Medical Sciences (AIIMS), Bhubaneshwar

New Century Publications
New Delhi, India

NEW CENTURY PUBLICATIONS
4800 / 24, Bharat Ram Road,
Ansari Road, Daryaganj,
New Delhi - 110 002 (India)

Tel.: 011 - 4358 7398, 4101 7798, 2324 7798

Email: info@newcenturypublications.com

www.newcenturypublications.com

Editorial office:
4832/24, Ansari Road, Daryaganj,
New Delhi – 110 002

Tel.: 011-4356 0919

First Published: **2020**

ISBN: **978-81-7708-517-4**

Published by New Century Publications and printed at Milan Enterprises, New Delhi.

Designs: Patch Creative Unit, New Delhi.

PRINTED IN INDIA

About the Book

With strong macroeconomic fundamentals, the Indian economy was well-placed on trajectory of high growth rate in early 2020 when outbreak of coronavirus epidemic in China was reported. On March 11, 2020, the World Health Organization (WHO) declared the epidemic as a pandemic, plunging the world into an unprecedented medical crisis.

When countrywide lockdown was announced from March 25, 2020, most of the economic activities came to a grinding halt in urban areas. However, rural India continued to be normal in view of the exemption from restrictions allowed to farmers to conduct farming operations, including harvesting and transporting their produce to grain markets with the general conditions of face covering, hand hygiene and social distancing. These exemptions helped to maintain continuity in supply chain, especially in view of harvesting and sowing season.

To deal with the economic challenges caused by the pandemic, Prime Minister Narendra Modi announced the creation of 'COVID-19 Economic Response Task Force' under the Union Finance Minister. Similarly, PM CARES Fund was created to deal with any kind of emergency or distress situation.

On May 12, 2020, the Prime Minister announced Aatmanirbhar Bharat Abhiyan (Self-reliant India Initiative) which combined relief, policy reforms and fiscal and monetary measures to help businesses and individuals to cope with the situation created by COVID-19 pandemic. A mega package of ₹ 20 lakh crore (10 percent of GDP) was announced for the purpose.

India has several strengths that can help mitigate the adverse effects of COVID-induced slowdown. Agricultural sector is vibrant, inflation is under control, foreign exchange reserves (more than US$ 500 billion) are at record level, international crude oil prices are low and a robust social security net is in place. There is, therefore, a silver lining for India to bounce back and a strong case for fast-tracking the pending reforms.

About the Authors

Dr. Niranjan Sahoo is Professor of Disaster Management, at Xavier Institute of Social Service (XISS), Ranchi. He is also Advisor, National Productivity Council, Ministry of Industry and Commerce, Government of India. Born in Odisha, he is academically specialized in rural management domain in general and disaster management in particular. In his 20-years of job experience, he initially got a campus placement offer while studying at Visva-Bharati University, Santiniketan by a Germany-based funding agency (EZE, Bonn) located in Calcutta. He was felicitated with Visva-Bharati Snatakattor Upadhi in 1997 at Santiniketan by the then Prime Minister of India Shri I.K. Gujral. He got his Ph.D. degree from Magadh University, Bodhgaya, India.

Professor Sahoo received International Intellectual Award 2010 in an International Conference on "Indo-Thai Friendship Summit and Economic Growth" held in Bangkok, Thailand on December 30, 2010 for outstanding rural development teachings. He has travelled to Nepal, US, Bangladesh, England, Singapore, South Korea, Indonesia, China, France, Switzerland, Thailand, Mongolia, Germany and Mexico for academic purposes. He has to his credit 15 research publications in national and international journals. Besides, he has authored three books, the recent one being annotated by *Journal of Economic Literature* of Economic Association of America and reviewed by the Prime Minister of India. Being a community member to the UNSDRR, he was part of the United Nations delegation to its global platform held in Mexico (2017), Ulaan Baatar (2018) and in Geneva (2019) along with the Home Minister of India.

Dr. Mukunda Chandra Sahoo is Associate Professor, Department of Hospital Administration, All India Institute of Medical Sciences (AIIMS), Bhubaneswar. He did his MBBS from MKCG Medical College, Berhampur and postgraduate studies in hospital administration from All India Institute of Medical Sciences, New Delhi. Dr. Sahoo is a hospital administrator with experience in hospital management and has served in various capacities in Indian Army, DRDO and healthcare organisations in the government sector. He is a research guide and examiner for postgraduate studies in hospital administration and has written a number of articles and book chapters on management of hospitals. His exemplary services were duly acknowledged by the Indian Army and DRDO. Currently, he is also Additional Medical Superintendent, AIIMS, Bhubaneshwar.

Contents

Preface

The year 2019 delivered a huge political mandate for the government. Real GDP growth for the year 2019-20 was projected at 7 percent, reflecting a recovery in the economy after a deceleration in the growth momentum throughout 2018-19. The growth in the economy was expected to pick up in 2019-20 as macroeconomic conditions continued to be stable while structural reforms initiated in the previous few years were continuing on course.

With strong macroeconomic fundamentals, the India economy was well-placed on trajectory of high growth rate in early 2020 when the news of coronavirus epidemic came from China. On March 11, 2020, the World Health Organization (WHO) declared the epidemic as a pandemic, plunging the world into an unprecedented crisis.

Normal economic activities around the world were disrupted. India announced stringent nationwide lockdown from March 25, 2020. The lockdown, in consecutive instalments, to slow down the spread of the disease, is expected to affect adversely and sharply the growth rate of the Indian economy during 2020-21 and beyond. There are fears that the economy may actually shrink.

Prime Minister Narendra Modi announced on May 12, 2020 the Aatmanirbhar Bharat Abhiyan which combined relief, policy reforms and fiscal and monetary measures to help businesses and individuals to cope with the situation created by COVID-19 pandemic. A mega package of ₹ 20 lakh crore (10 percent of GDP) was announced for the purpose.

The details of the ₹ 20 lakh crore package were announced by Finance Minister Nirmala Sitharaman in five tranches during the next five consecutive days. All the measures were aimed at spurring investment and buffering the economy against the Covid pandemic shock.

The first tranche, announced on May 13, 2020, was focused on micro, small and medium enterprises (MSMEs) which were badly hit by the medical crisis.

The second tranche, announced on May 14, 2020, gave relief to the poor and lower middle class.

The third tranche, announced on May 15, 2020, pertained to a mix of financial, legislative and other reform measures aimed largely at increasing the pricing power of farmers.

The fourth tranche, announced on May 16, 2020, related to measures which included a major opening up of coal, defence production, civil aviation, power, space, social infrastructure and atomic energy for private participation.

The fifth tranche, announced on May 17, 2020, focus mainly on Mahatma Gandhi National Rural Employment Guarantee Scheme (MGNREGS)—the flagship rural job guarantee scheme of the Central Government.

Post-COVID, uncertainty is reigning supreme and countries are thinking of self-sufficiency. World economies are unsure as to what extent they can depend on others in the future.

Everyone is now agreed that the way forward is too uncertain. It is not possible to clearly see the path over the foreseeable future. It is just not possible to have a precise road map all laid out to be unfolded in one go.

Compared to other developing economies, India has several strengths that can help mitigate the adverse effects of COVID-induced slowdown. The Government has taken several measures in this direction and the economy is expected to return to the high growth trajectory. Sustained interest in India as a long-term investment destination and a comfortable foreign exchange reserve position suggest that the external sector can continue to support stability and growth. As the monetary and fiscal stimuli work their way through, and if calm and confidence are restored in the global markets, India can see economic turn around soon.

August 2020 **Niranjan Sahoo**

1

Pre- and Post-COVID World Economy

After the globalization wave starting early 1980s and the establishment of World Trade Organization (WTO) in 1995, almost all economies of the world are dovetailed with each other and India is no exception. What happens at the global level has repercussions for the domestic economy of a country. Recessionary tendencies in global economy adversely affect individual economies and a boom has the positive effects.

The nature of world economy, and the role of the governments in it, has undergone a paradigm shift. Driven by an increasingly open and liberalized structure, private sector has matured into a vibrant and dynamic force, operating not just at the international cutting edge, but also with a global scale and reach. This changed economic landscape requires a new administrative paradigm in which the role of government must evolve from simply allocating resources in a command and control economic system, to a far more nuanced one of directing, calibrating, supporting and regulating a market-oriented economic system.

Government must thus transit from being a provider of first and last resort and major player in the economy, to being a catalyst nurturing an enabling environment, where the entrepreneurial spirits—from self-employed entrepreneurs to large corporations—can flourish. Today, we live in a *global village*, connected by modern transport, communications and media, and networked international markets and institutions. In the current global dynamics, a country is also influenced by happenings far removed from its borders.

1.1 Pre-COVID World Economy

For the global economy, the year 2018 was difficult, with the world output growth falling from 3.8 percent in 2017 to 3.6

percent in 2018. Growth rate of world output was projected to fall further to 3.3 percent in 2019 as growth rates of both advanced economies and emerging and developing economies are expected to decline.

The global macroeconomic landscape was chartering a rough and uncertain terrain characterized by weak growth of world output. The situation was exacerbated by: (a) declining prices of a number of commodities, with reduction in crude oil prices being the most visible of them, (b) turbulent financial markets (more so equity markets), and (c) volatile exchange rates. These conditions reflected extreme risk-aversion behaviour of global investors, thus putting many, and in particular, commodities exporting economies, under considerable stress.

1.1.1 Weak Recovery from Financial Crisis of 2008: Financial turmoil which surfaced in August 2007 in the US financial system—as a result of defaults of sub-prime mortgage loans—blew into an unprecedented financial crisis engulfing international money, credit, equity and foreign exchange markets. It was preceded by an extended phase of buoyant world economy characterized by output expansion, burgeoning world trade, favourable financial and economic conditions, liquidity overhang and low interest rates. Economists termed it as a period of Great Moderation.

The Great Moderation soon turned into Great Dismay when global financial confusion—simmering since August 2007—began unleashing its full fury in September 2008 with a series of failures of major financial institutions. The crisis traversed from the financial to the real sector and it looked like that the recession—which was still keeping world governments on tenterhooks—would be deeper and the recovery longer than earlier anticipated.

Recovery in the global economy was proceeding albeit at a modest pace and often falling short of forecasts. A decade after the financial and economic crisis, the global output gap was still substantial, the markets continued to be shaky, and the future was overshadowed by severe political risks. Due to high uncertainties, public and private investments remained subdued in most parts of the world.

The pace of recovery varied from one economic region to another. Some economies—such as the United States and the United Kingdom—were above their pre-crisis output levels, while others—such as the Euro zone and Japan—were not. Emerging economies remained the locomotive of global growth, though there were differences among them. Although decelerating, growth was still robust in China, weak in Russia and Brazil while it was strong in India, Indonesia, and South Africa. Oil-producing and exporting countries like Russia, Saudi Arabia, Nigeria, Iran and Venezuela were adversely affected by sliding crude prices. Conversely, the drop in global oil prices provided a substantial stimulus to the economies of net-oil-importing countries, viz. Turkey, Korea, China, and India.

One of the reasons making the recovery process ineffectual was that trade was weak by historical standards. The weak recovery of world economy was also attributable to rising protectionism. According to the WTO, there was a significant increase in restrictive trade measures introduced by G20 economies since 2008. Import tariffs had remained low but regulatory burdens and non-tariff barriers—including onerous environmental and safety standards—impeded international trade.

1.1.2 Falling Crude Oil Prices: Swing producer Saudi Arabia—world's biggest crude exporter—had consistently refused to heed appeals from OPEC (Organization for Petroleum Exporting Countries) members, in particular Iran and Venezuela, to arrest the decline in oil prices by cutting production.

Glut in the market was also attributable to rising supplies from new players such as US shale industry and Russia. US was using the technology of horizontal fracturing to extract shale oil and gas, and slowly reducing its dependence on crude.

Weakening of Chinese and European economies had also reduced the demand for crude. The Eurozone's economic growth was anaemic and no amount of monetary easing was helping it to revive growth. Weak demand and sharp decreases in oil and other raw materials prices were keeping inflation low in many OECD (Organization for Economic Co-operation and Development) economies pointing to the risk of deflation in some countries. However in energy-importing countries, the decline in oil prices offered a growth premium and an improvement in current account imbalances.

1.1.3 International Trade: The Doha Round of trade negotiations in the WTO which began in 2001 remained unfinished due to differences among members on various issues. The scope of Doha Round of negotiations included agriculture, market access for non-agricultural products, services trade, trade-related aspects of intellectual property rights (TRIPS), rules (covering anti-dumping and subsidies), trade facilitation and so on. The conduct, conclusion and entry into force of the outcome of the negotiations were parts of a single undertaking, that is, *nothing is agreed until everything is agreed.*

The Doha Round had made very little progress after 2008. Throughout 2009 and 2010, discussions continued but no headway was made on any substantive issue in the negotiations. However, the subject featured on the agenda of almost every major international meeting and there were strong affirmations of political support for an early conclusion of the Doha Round. Discussions continued in Geneva during March and April 2011, in a variety of formats. Reports on each area of the negotiations were issued on April 21, 2011. These documents provided an overview of the status of negotiations in each area covered in the Doha Development Agenda. While they indicated significant progress in many areas, they also captured the wide gaps remaining on many issues.

Progress was very slow due to wide gaps in the expectations of the members. There were several attempts to bring the talks back on track and to build on the results already achieved in the negotiations. There were constant attempts in the WTO and in other forums like the G20 to resolve the impasse. During the Ministerial Conference of the WTO held in December 2011, members once again reaffirmed their belief in rule-based multilateral trade and their commitment to resolve the issues in a transparent way through consensus.

The prolonged hiatus in the Doha Round talks was a matter of concern. It was not for want of willingness on the part of developing countries to engage, but was the result of an apparent perception among some developed countries that they would not gain much from the Round. The neglect of the Doha Round was unfortunate and jeopardised an opportunity to strengthen multilateral trade rules.

Because progress in trade negotiations at the WTO remained stalled, many countries were turning their attention to plurilateral and regional trading arrangements (RTAs) as second-best options for opening markets. Mega-initiatives, such as the Transpacific Partnership (TPP), the Transatlantic Trade and Investment Partnership (TTIP), and the Regional Comprehensive Economic Partnership (RCEP) among ASEAN countries, had the potential to address essential trade policy questions across a much wider geographical scope.

1.1.4 Geo-political Tensions and Protracted Geo-political Turmoil: Besides economic and financial risks, the world faced elevated geo-political risks. Global economic growth was threatened by high political risks and uncertainties posed by conflicts in East Europe, North Africa, Middle East, and East Asia. With the demise of the *de-coupling hypothesis,* uncertainties in conflict zones were transmitted to other economies of the world. Geo-political turmoil caused a significant risk to financial markets and growth besides immense human suffering.

1.1.5 Exchange Rate and Capital Market Volatility: The emerging markets faced the risk of renewed market volatility due to the exit from monetary easing in the US. The anticipated changes in the US monetary policy led to growing concerns about a sudden shift in investor sentiment and ensuing disruptive asset price corrections. The US dollar was appreciating against the euro and currencies of several emerging market economies (EMEs). Apart from the US, serious instability and volatility in exchange rates were being driven by policymakers in the developed world who were seeking to boost exports by weakening their own currencies.

1.1.6 Financial System Problems and Debt: The resilience of the financial sector had improved after the financial crisis. However, in some countries deleveraging and recapitalization were not finished and non-performing loans were still high, making the banking sector vulnerable to adverse shocks. Those vulnerabilities, in some cases, led to liquidity problems if the stress in financial markets increased.

Highly accommodative monetary policy had led to greater risk-taking and recorded highs in some asset prices. Uncertainties pertaining to the world economy, risk aversion and tougher regulatory standards created demand for safe assets. This was nurturing financial market vulnerabilities and creating concerns about a sudden shift in investor sentiment and consequently disruptive asset price corrections.

1.1.7 Unemployment: All countries faced the same challenge of increasing the pace of job creation and, wherever possible, improving the quality of jobs. Although the situation had improved somewhat, unemployment remained a key concern. Even for people who still had jobs, working conditions had deteriorated. Youth unemployment was a bigger concern.

Another concern in the labour markets was that labour force participation was not growing as rapidly as before and this put a cap on potential growth. Declining labour force participation was a result of lower population growth but also because of discouraged workers. A sizeable number of people had disappeared from the labour force because they had given up looking for work.

Lower real wages created a barrier to accelerating growth in advanced countries. Declining real wages had helped to contain the degree of unemployment and restore competitiveness only in some specific cases.

The world was also grappling with following issues and concerns:

1. Achieving high levels of nuclear safety.
2. Maintaining a rules-based maritime order and achieving maritime security
3. Strengthening the system of multilateral treaties/arms trade treaty.
4. Fighting trafficking of migrants and tackling causes for refugee crises.
5. Protecting marine environment.
6. Ensuring food security.
7. Dealing with climate change
8. Fighting terrorism and its financing.

Above was the global scenario when news of coronavirus epidemic came from China. On March 11, 2020, the World Health Organization (WHO) declared the epidemic as a pandemic, plunging the world into an unprecedented crisis.

1.2 Post-COVID World Economy

Post-COVID, global economy has come to a screeching halt. There is tremendous loss of production, income and employment. According to International Monetary Fund (IMF), world economy is expected to shrink by 3 percent in 2020. On April 28, 2020, Moody's Investors Services projected that all G-20 advanced economies would contract by 5.8 percent in 2020.

On June 8, 2020, World Bank released its report titled *Global Economic Prospects* and predicted that world economy would shrink by 5.2 percent in 2020. Advanced economies would experience growth falling by 7 percent while emerging economies (including India) as a group would see a growth decline of 2.5 percent. According to the report, Indian economy would shrink by 3.2 percent in the fiscal year 2020-21. The report, which contained an assessment of economic shocks from coronavirus pandemic shutdowns, noted that the pandemic has plunged the world into a severe recession, deepest since the Second World War.

In the wake of COVID-19, most countries of the world resorted to lockdowns, resulting in cessation of almost all economic activities.

Although many countries have gradually lifted restrictions to restart their economies, the situation is not likely to return to pre-Covid period soon due to following reasons:

1. Tariff barriers and tariff wars among nations, particularly between US and China.
2. Protectionist policies.
3. Turbulent financial markets.
4. Geo-political tensions, particularly between US and Iran, Turkish invasion of Syria, civil war in Yemen.

These conditions reflect extreme risk-aversion behaviour of global investors, thus putting many economies under considerable stress. The dynamics for a strong, sustainable, balanced and inclusive growth will probably remain weak in the foreseeable future.

Finally, an overhaul of the world's financial system—led by World Bank and International Monetary Fund (IMF)—is overdue as was the case with General Agreement on Tariffs and Trade GATT which was superseded by World Trade Organisation (WTO) in 1995.

2

Pre- and Post-COVID Indian Economy

2.1 Pre-COVID Indian Economy

2.1.1 GDP Growth Rate: India recorded an average annual growth rate of 7.2 percent during the first five-year term of Prime Minister Narendra Modi. GDP growth was adversely impacted in the last two years (2017-18 and 2018-19) of the first term of Modi Government by the following two important events:

1. Demonetization of high denomination currency notes on November 8, 2016. [1]
2. Introduction of Goods and Services Tax (GST) with effect from July 1, 2017. [2]

The above measures disrupted the economy in the short-run. GDP growth fell to below 7 percent (6.6 percent and 6.8 percent in 2017-18 and 2018-19 respectively), dragging the overall five-year growth average down from a putative 8 percent to 7.2 percent. The 6.8 percent growth in 2018-19 (as against the expected 7.2 percent) was attributed to slow growth of agriculture and manufacturing. However, India still remained the fastest growing major economy in the world.

With the shock treatment to the economy administered by demonetisation (to digitise the financial ecosystem) and GST (to coalesce multiple state-level taxes) more or less over, GDP growth was expected to return to its 2014-15 to 2016-17 trend line of 7.5-8 percent. Hiccups over, it was now time to reap the benefits of demonetization and GST.

Table 2.1 presents GDP growth rates for the recent years. [3] It is noticeable that the growth rate in 2013-14 (last year of the UPA-II rule) was 6.6 percent. Growth rate was never below this figure during the first five-year term of Prime Minister Narendra Modi.

Table 2.1: Real GDP Growth Rates in Recent Period

(percent)

Period	GDP growth
2013-14	6.6
2014-15	7.2
2015-16	7.6
2016-17	7.1
2017-18	6.6
2018-19	6.8
2019-20	4.2

The year 2019 delivered a huge political mandate for the government. Real GDP growth for the year 2019-20 was projected at 7 percent, reflecting a recovery in the economy after a deceleration in the growth momentum throughout 2018-19. The growth in the economy was expected to pick up in 2019-20 as macroeconomic conditions continued to be stable while structural reforms initiated in the previous few years were continuing on course.

The economic slowdown precipitated a debate on the primacy of cyclical versus structural factors for the disturbing trends. Government was not oblivious of the slowdown as was evidenced by the measures it took to boost the economy.

2.1.2 Measures to Boost the Economy: On August 23, 2019, Government announced a range of measures to boost economic sentiments, improve availability of credit and working capital and provide some sort of stimulus to the automobile sector. Withdrawal of surcharge on long-term capital gains was also announced.

On August 26, 2019, RBI, in a historic move, transferred ₹ 1.76 lakh crore surplus reserve to the Government. It was meant to help the Government in reducing financial stress on the economy and contain fiscal deficit as well.

Many economists termed the move as a *lifeline* for the Government which was exploring options to revive economic growth amid a period of sluggish consumer demand and weak investments.

RBI decided to transfer this record high surplus after approving all the recommendations of the Bimal Jalan-led expert committee, which was constituted to decide the size of capital reserves that the central bank should hold.

Before the RBI's announcement, the Government had budgeted ₹ 90,000 crore as surplus and dividend transfers from RBI for the current fiscal (2019-20). However, it got ₹ 86,000 crore more than the budgeted amount.

On August 28, another package was announced which included liberalization of FDI in coal and digital media. On August 30, 2019, the Government announced the mega merger of public sector banks to modernise the financial sector.

On September 14, 2019, Government announced a package for real estate and export sector. It announced the creation of a ₹ 20,000 crore fund for real estate projects that was expected to help complete around 3,50,000 flats and houses stuck in various stages of completion. Government also announced the introduction of a new scheme for reimbursement of taxes paid on exports. The scheme called the Remission of Duties and Taxes on Export Products came into effect from January 2020, entailing a loss of revenue to the tune of ₹ 50,000.

2.1.3 Fiscal Stimulus: On September 20, 2019 Government announced a hefty fiscal stimulus for the corporate sector by reducing the corporate tax rate for domestic manufacturing from 30 percent to 22 percent and for new manufacturing companies from 25 percent to 15 percent. The announcement spurred the stock market instantly when BSE Sensex soared 1921 points—the highest single day rise in a decade. The tax cuts became effective retrospectively from April 1, 2019. These tax slashes were expected to allow Indian companies to compete with those in lower-tax jurisdictions globally and also to attract significant investments from abroad.

2.1.4 Improved Ranking on Various Indices: In terms of ease of doing business, India improved its ranking from 142 in 2015 to 63 in 2020, a jump of 79 spots. [4]

India, which was ranked 81 in the 2015 Global Innovation

Index (GII) published by World Intellectual Property Organization (WIPO), went up to 66th spot in 2016, 60th in 2017, 57th in 2018 and 52nd in 2019. Thus, India jumped 29 notches in four years. Similarly, India entered for the first time in the list of 60 countries for which data was published in the Bloomberg Innovation Index, 2019 report. As a debutant, India occupied 54th position in the index prepared and published by Bloomberg, New York-based media firm. [5]

In the World Digital Competitiveness Ranking prepared by International Institute for Management Development, Lausanne (Switzerland), India moved up four places to 44th rank in 2019 as compared to 48th rank in 2018. Its position in 2019 improved overall in all factors including knowledge, technology and future readiness in exploring more digital technologies. India's biggest improvement in 2019 was in the technology sub-factor level, where it held the first position in telecommunications investment. [6]

According to the 2018 survey by The Economist Intelligence Unit, commissioned by payments company Visa, India was taking rapid strides in advancing government e-payments capabilities and was one of the top-performing countries in terms of citizen-to-government (C2G), business-to-government (B2G) and government-to-business (G2B) transactions.

The country held the top ranking on B2G and G2B, and comes third on C2G jointly with Argentina. In the 73-country survey, India's overall ranking on government's adoption of e-payments moved up to 28th in 2018, from 36th in 2011. According to the survey, India could further improve its standing by focusing on expanding access to digital infrastructure, investing in socio-economic development, and promoting a healthy, competitive market. [7]

In the *Travel and Tourism Competitiveness Report, 2019,* published by the World Economic Forum, India was placed at 34th position among 140 countries of the world. India showed the greatest percentage improvement to its overall score, helping it to become the only low-middle income country in the top 35.

India was ranked at 52nd place (among 141 countries) in the 2015 Report and at 40th place (among 136 countries) in the 2017 Report. Thus, India jumped 18 spots in 4 years (from 52nd in 2015 to 34th in 2019) and 6 spots in 2 years (from 40th in 2017 to 34th in 2019). Cultural heritage and natural resources were two factors where India scored highly in the Report. The country also worked on its business environment and environmental sustainability.

India's growth story had largely remained positive on the strength of domestic absorption, and the country was registering a robust and steady pace of economic growth in recent years. Additionally, its other macroeconomic parameters like inflation, fiscal deficit and current account balance had exhibited distinct signs of improvement. However, weak growth in advanced and emerging economies had taken its toll on India's exports. As imports had also declined, principally on account of reduced prices of crude oil for which the country is heavily dependent on imports, trade and current account deficits continued to be moderate.

IMF had praised India for implementing important reforms including introduction of GST, inflation targeting and Insolvency and Bankruptcy Code.

With all the above favourable factors for rapid economic growth, outbreak of coronavirus epidemic in China was reported. On March 11, 2020, the world Health Organization (WHO) declared the epidemic as a pandemic. Normal economic activities around the world were disrupted. India announced a stringent nationwide lockdown from March 25, 2020.

2.2 Post-COVID Indian Economy

Data released by the NSO on May 29, 2020 showed that Indian economy grew by 4.2 percent in 2019-20 on the back of falling investment and consumption. This was against the projected figure of 5 percent. The 4.2 percent rate was the lowest in the last 11 years.

Similarly, it grew by 3.1 percent in the fourth quarter

(January, February and March) of 2019-20, again against the estimated figure of 4.7 percent. The 3.1 percent rate was the lowest since March 2009 when, under the impact of sub-prime global financial crisis, the economy expanded by merely 0.2 percent.

As the countrywide lockdown was imposed from March 25, 2020 in the wake of coronavirus disease (COVID-19), the data did not reflect the impact of lockdown and was purely the result of *business-as-usual* factors.

The lockdown, in consecutive instalments, to slow down the spread of the disease, is expected to affect adversely and sharply the growth rate of the Indian economy during 2020-21 and beyond. There are fears that the economy may actually shrink.

Post-COVID, Moody's forecast (on April 28, 2020) for India for calendar year 2020 is 0.2 percent. For G-20 developed countries it is -5 percent.

On June 8, 2020, World Bank released its report titled *Global Economic Prospects* and predicted that world economy would shrink by 5.2 percent in 2020. Advanced economies would experience growth falling by 7 percent while emerging economies (including India) as a group would see a growth decline of 2.5 percent. According to the report, Indian economy would shrink by 3.2 percent in the fiscal year 2020-21.

The country is going through an unprecedented crisis owing to COVID pandemic. Nations across the globe have gone into lockdown and people are struggling to find ways to fight the disease and its spread. Social distancing, hand hygiene and face covering have become the new norms of life.

India was one of the first countries to put up a concerted, comprehensive action plan to stop the spread of the virus and limit the number of infections. World Health Organization (WHO) praised the efforts made by the Indian Government to fight the pandemic. India was one of the few countries which announced a complete lockdown even before the COVID cases in the country were less than 1,000. When the medical crisis started, people demonstrated their full commitment in preventing its spread.

2.2.1 PM CARES Fund and Aatmanirbhar Bharat Abhiyan: To deal with the economic challenges caused by the pandemic, the Prime Minister announced the creation of 'COVID-19 Economic Response Task Force' under the Union Finance Minister. Similarly, PM CARES Fund was created which deals with any kind of emergency or distress situation like a public health emergency or any other kind of emergency, calamity or distress, either manmade or natural

On March 13, 2020, the Central Government announced 4 percent increase in dearness allowance (DA) for its employees and pensioners with effect from January 1, 2020. Considering the calamitous situation created by coronavirus, the Government, on April 23, announced the freezing of DA payment, clarifying that the move was temporary. DA is paid to adjust the cost of living against inflation. Presumably, the Government's intention was to divert a part of available funds at its disposal towards more urgent needs of the corona-stricken and other vulnerable citizens of the country.

Similarly, remuneration of Members of Parliament was reduced by 30 percent for a year.

On May 12, 2020, the Prime Minister announced a ₹ 20 lakh crore stimulus package which was about 10 percent of GDP. It was named as Aatmanirbhar Bharat Abhiyan (Self-reliant India Initiative). [8]

2.2.2 FDI Policy Tweaked to Curb Opportunistic Acquisition of Firms Amid Covid-19: On April 18, 2020, the Ministry of Commerce and Industry, Government of India, revised its foreign direct investment (FDI) policy intending to curb takeovers or acquisitions of Indian companies during the ongoing coronavirus pandemic.

According to the revised policy any investment by an entity of a country that shares a land border with India or where the beneficial owner of investment is a citizen of any of those countries will need government approval. Earlier, only Bangladesh and Pakistan were under this category, which was expanded to all neighbouring countries sharing the border with India. India shares land borders with seven neighbouring countries of Pakistan, Bangladesh, China, Nepal, Myanmar, Bhutan, and Afghanistan.

Further, any transfer in the ownership of any such existing or future FDI will also require the government's approval.

This was done amid a rising concern across the globe that Chinese companies were investing in those firms that had been severely hit in the wake of the COVID-19 outbreak.

Meanwhile, the Chinese Embassy in India issued a statement pointing out that the revised FDI policy would make it difficult for companies from countries sharing land borders with India, including China, to invest in the country.

India did not name China, but it was obvious that the move was aimed at preventing hostile takeovers by Chinese companies of Indian firms whose market values have dipped because of COVID-19 related uncertainties.

To curb the COVID-19 outbreak in the country, the Indian government has taken several initiatives and measures to boost the economy in these testing times.

Everyone is now agreed that the way forward is too uncertain. It is not possible to clearly see the path over the foreseeable future. It is just not possible to have a precise road map all laid out to be unfolded in one go. Given the unpredictable and volatile international situation, almost every country has to manage under uncertainty. In the circumstances, Government should be prepared to respond to the evolving situation swiftly and effectively, and to the extent possible, in anticipation of immediate developments.

Similarly, there are indications that protectionist tendencies have increased around the world in anticipation of the growing possibilities of slower growth in advanced economies.

Over the years, India has built an extensive network of social safety-net programmes, including the flagship Mahatma Gandhi National Rural Employment Guarantee Scheme

(MGNREGS). These uniquely Indian versions of automatic stabilizers should protect the poor from the extreme impact of COVID pandemic.

Any assessment of the performance of the Indian economy and its current status has to be made in the context of developments in the global economy. India is a major player in international economic affairs, particularly in terms of consumer market. International trade and investment are moderating, trade tensions remain elevated, and financing conditions are tightening. Amid recent episodes of financial stress, growth in emerging market and developing economies has lost momentum. Financial market pressures and trade tensions can escalate, denting global activity.

Compared to other developing economies, India has several strengths that can help mitigate the adverse effects of COVID-induced slowdown. The Government has taken several measures in this direction and the economy is expected to return to the high growth trajectory. Sustained interest in India as a long-term investment destination and a comfortable foreign exchange reserve position suggest that the external sector can continue to support stability and growth. As the monetary and fiscal stimuli work their way through, and if calm and confidence are restored in the global markets, India can see economic turn around soon. The high growth *miracle economies* of Asia were able to maintain their high growth for decades despite repeated shocks, as they responded quickly and effectively to counter these shocks through pragmatic policies. There is, therefore, a silver lining for India and a strong case for fast-tracking pending reforms.

Endnotes

1. In a historical move to fight against the evils of black money, corruption, money laundering, financing of terrorists and counterfeit notes, the Government of India decided to withdraw the legal tender character of ₹ 500 and ₹ 1,000 banknotes of the Mahatma Gandhi Series from the midnight of November 8, 2016. The announcement was made by no less a person than the

Prime Minister Narendra Modi himself in an unscheduled live televised address to the nation on the evening of November 8, 2016.

Short-term costs took the form of inconvenience and hardships, especially to those in the informal and cash-intensive sectors of the economy who lost income and employment. Analysts generally held the view that the demonetization move of the Government would hit the economy hard in the short-term but benefit it in the long-run.

2. India introduced a comprehensive Goods and Services Tax (GST) on July 1, 2017. Prior to the introduction of GST, the indirect tax system of India suffered from various disabilities. There was a burden of *tax-on-tax* in the pre-GST system of Central excise duty and the sales tax (later VAT) system of the States.

   GST is a tax on goods and services with comprehensive and continuous chain of set-off benefits up to the retailer level. It is essentially a tax only on value addition at each stage, and a supplier at each stage is permitted to set-off, through a tax credit mechanism, the GST paid on the purchase of goods and services. Ultimately, the burden of GST is borne by the end-user (i.e. final consumer) of the commodity/service.

3. GDP is defined as the money value of goods and services produced in an economy during a year. In India, estimates of GDP growth are released, through a press note, on quarterly basis by National Statistical Office (NSO)—a wing of the Ministry of Statistics and Programme Implementation—on the last working day of the second month following the quarter. Thus, data for the last quarter (January to March) of 2019-20 was released on May 29, 2020. The press note also announces the date of the next release of quarterly GDP estimates. Following estimates are provided:

- Estimates of GDP at constant prices (2011-12).
- Estimates of GDP at current prices.
- Estimates of gross value added (GVA) at constant prices (2011-12).
- Estimates of GVA at current prices.
- Estimates of expenditure components of GDP.

4. For details, see chapter 8 of this book.
5. For details of both the Global Innovation Index (GII) and

Bloomberg Innovation Index, see chapter 10 of this book.

6. For details, see chapter 11 of this book.
7. For details, see chapter 11 of this book.
8. See chapter 4 of this book for Aatmanirbhar Bharat Abhiyan.

3

India's US$ 5 Trillion Economy Dream Shattered

It was in January 2018 in Davos (Switzerland) that Prime Minister Narendra Modi first expressed his ambition to make India a 5 trillion dollar economy by 2024-25. He reiterated the target at Governing Council Meeting of NITI Aayog in New Delhi in June 2019. [1]

In her speech to the Parliament while presenting the Budget for 2019-20 (Final) on July 5, 2019, Finance Minister Nirmala Sitharaman emphatically asserted, "Our economy was at approximately US$ 1.85 trillion when we formed the Government in 2014. Within 5 years it has reached US$ 2.7 trillion. Hence, it is well within our capacity to reach the US$ 5 trillion in the next few years." She further said, "The Indian economy will grow to become a 3 trillion dollar economy in the current year (2019-20). It is now the sixth largest in the world. Five years ago, it was at the 11th position". [2]

In her speech to the Parliament while presenting the Budget for 2020-21 on February 1, 2020, she declared India as the "fifth largest economy of the world" (after US, China, Japan and Germany).

3.1 Twelve Champion Services Sectors

In December 2018, Ministry of Commerce and Industry, Government of India released an action-oriented plan which highlighted specific sector level interventions to bolster India's march towards becoming a US$ 5 trillion economy before 2025. The plan was focused on boosting services sector contribution to US$ 3 trillion, manufacturing to US$ 1 trillion and agriculture to US$ 1 trillion. The Ministry created a corpus of US$ 1 billion to boost *twelve champion sectors* in services and it was working on releasing the New Industrial Policy keeping in mind the demands of the future.

The twelve identified champion services sectors for promoting their development, and realizing their potential were as under:

1. Information technology (IT) and IT-enabled services.
2. Tourism and hospitality services.
3. Medical value travel.
4. Transport and logistics services.
5. Accounting and finance services.
6. Audio-visual services.
7. Legal services.
8. Communication services.
9. Construction and related engineering services.
10. Environmental services.
11. Financial services.
12. Educational services.

This initiative was envisaged to enhance the competitiveness of India's services sector through the implementation of focused and monitored Action Plans, thereby promoting GDP growth, creating more jobs and promoting exports to global markets. Services sector in India has immense employment potential.

3.2 Blueprint for the 5 Trillion Dollar Economy

Drawing a blueprint for the next 5 years, *Economic Survey, 2018-19* stated, "To achieve the objective of becoming a US$ 5 trillion economy by 2024-25, India needs to sustain a real GDP growth rate of 8 percent. International experience, especially from high-growth East Asian economies, suggests that such growth can only be sustained by a *virtuous cycle* of savings, investment and exports catalysed and supported by a favourable demographic phase. Investment, especially private investment, is the 'key driver' that drives demand, creates capacity, increases labour productivity, introduces new technology, allows creative destruction, and generates jobs.

Exports must form an integral part of the growth model because higher savings preclude domestic demand as the driver of final demand". [3]

Economic Survey, 2018-19, assumed an average real annual growth rate in GDP of 8 percent from 2020-21 to 2024-25. It also assumed an inflation rate of 4 percent. This implied a nominal growth rate of 12 percent.

Further, it assumed an exchange rate of ₹ 75 per dollar in March 2025. Based on these assumptions, it was estimated that the Indian economy must have a nominal GDP of ₹ 375 lakh crores in March 2025. [4] ₹ 375 lakh crore were converted into dollar 5 lakh crore (at ₹ 75 per dollar). Dollar 5 lakh crore = Dollar 5 trillion (since 1 lakh crore = 1 trillion).

If the 5 trillion dollar dream had translated into reality, India would have been the world's fourth-largest economy in 2024-25, only behind U.S., China and Japan.

Apparently, the following three variables were involved in the above calculations.

1. Real GDP growth rate of 8 percent per annum to be achieved through savings, investment, exports and favourable demographic phase.
2. Inflation rate of 4 percent per annum. Inflation rate had been hovering around 3.5 percent at that time. Even global inflation was not very high.
3. Exchange rate of ₹ 75 per dollar in March 2025. Rupee-dollar exchange rate needed to be in check to make India reach the desired target of 5 trillion dollar economy. Union Budget 2019-20 had proposed to issue an overseas sovereign bond in September 2019 to mop up US$ 10 billion through sovereign bonds overseas. This would have drawn additional foreign exchange. All of this could render projection of an exchange rate of ₹ 75 to a dollar in 2024-25 relatively realistic. There was every likelihood of external value of rupee remaining stable over the long-term.

Economic Survey, 2018-19, devoted an entire chapter to

behavioural economics that enunciated four major tactics to implement public policy:

1. **Laissez-faire:** Leaving individuals/firms to follow their own course.
2. **Nudge:** Gently steering people to a desired goal.
3. **Incentivise:** Using positive and negative inducements to change behaviour.
4. **Mandate:** Using diktat to enforce a particular outcome.

Government was employing all the four drivers of change to achieve the goal of 5 trillion dollar economy. Well-off Indians were asked to think in terms of *contributing to*, rather than *claiming from*, the national pool of goods and services.

With the microeconomic and macroeconomic foundations strong, the Indian economy was ready to shift gears so that economic growth, jobs and exports could be pushed up to the next level.

India is projected to be the world's most populous country by 2025, with at least 1.45 billion people. Given the geographic and demographic size of the country, a 5 trillion dollar economy by 2024-25 was the minimum to aspire for.

When all was going well, the news of coronavirus came from China. All countries of the world were alerted. On March 11, 2020, the World Health Organization (WHO) declared coronavirus epidemic as a pandemic.

On March 24, 2020 Prime Minister Narendra Modi, in a televised address to the nation, announced a stringent countrywide lockdown from March 25 to April 14 which was extended to May 3, to May 17, to May 31 and further to June but with gradual relaxations. Lockdowns were declared in most of the countries for varying periods to cope with the medical crisis. Global economy came to a grinding halt

In India, all transport movements (railways, airways, metros, road transport) were halted. Business establishments were closed down. The supply of essential goods and services only was allowed. The severity of the lockdown can be gauged from the fact that not a single motor vehicle was sold in the country during the month of April 2020. Gross GST collections which totalled ₹ 1,05,366 crore in the month of February fell to ₹ 97,597 crore in March and further down to ₹ 43,000 crore in April 2020. The country is going through an unprecedented crisis owing to COVID pandemic.

Endnotes

1. Trillion (thousand billion) = 1,000,000,000,000 = 10 *kharab* = 1 lakh crore.
2. Government of India, Ministry of Finance, Budget Papers 2019-20 (Final), *Speech of Minister of Finance*, July 5, 2019, paras 6 and 8.
3. Government of India, Ministry of Finance, *Economic Survey, 2018-19*, Volume I, p. 1.
4. Ibid., p. 4.

4

Aatmanirbhar Bharat Abhiyan (Self-reliant India Initiative)

Prime Minister Narendra Modi announced on May 12, 2020, the Aatmanirbhar Bharat Abhiyan which combined relief, policy reforms and fiscal and monetary measures to help businesses and individuals to cope with the situation created by Covid-19 pandemic. A mega package of ₹ 20 lakh crore (10 percent of GDP) was announced for the purpose. This included ₹ 1.7 lakh crore welfare package announced on March 26, 2020 under the Pradhan Mantri Garib Kalyan Yojana (PMGKY) to provide 3 LPG cylinders free (April, May and June) to over 8 crore beneficiaries of the Pradhan Mantri Ujjawala Yojana (PMUY). It also included monetary measures announced by Reserve Bank of India (RBI) during March-April 2020 which were estimated to be of the order of 5.2 lakh crore.

The details of the ₹ 20 lakh crore package were announced by Finance Minister Nirmala Sitharaman in five tranches during the next five consecutive days. All the measures were aimed at spurring investment and buffering the economy against the Covid pandemic shock.

The first tranche, announced on May 13, 2020, was focused on micro, small and medium enterprises (MSMEs) which were badly hit by the medical crisis.

The second tranche, announced on May 14, 2020, gave relief to the poor and lower middle class.

The third tranche, announced on May 15, 2020, pertained to a mix of financial, legislative and other reform measures aimed largely at increasing the pricing power of farmers.

The fourth tranche, announced on May 16, 2020, related to measures which included a major opening up of coal, defence production, civil aviation, power, space, social infrastructure and atomic energy for private participation.

The fifth tranche, announced on May 17, 2020, focused mainly on Mahatma Gandhi National Rural Employment Guarantee Scheme (MGNREGS)—the flagship rural job guarantee scheme of the Central Government.

4.1 First Tranche Focused on MSMEs

It was particularly challenging time for micro, small and medium enterprises (MSMEs) which were reeling under the harsh impact of the COVID pandemic. With manufacturing units being shut for a considerable period of time and migrant labourers also returning home, many of the MSMEs were on the brink of closing down all operations. In a bid to make this crucial sector of the economy survive, the Finance Minister in her first tranche of the stimulus laid out specific boosters that could offer some relief to this hard-hit sector. The nearly ₹ 6 lakh crore tranche, announced on May 13, 2020, included ₹ 3 lakh crore collateral-free automatic loans for MSMEs. Components of the first tranche are presented in Table 4.1.

4.1.1 New Classification and Definitions of MSMEs: Vide notification No. S.O. 1702 (E) dated June 1, 2020 and effective from July 1, 2020 of the Ministry of Micro, Small and Medium Enterprises, Government of India, the criterion for classification of micro, small and medium enterprises under Micro, Small and Medium Enterprises Development Act, 2006 was drastically liberalized.

Prior to July 1, 2020, MSMEs were classified into two classes:

1. **Manufacturing Enterprises:** Enterprises engaged in the manufacture or production of goods pertaining to any industry specified in the First Schedule of the Industries Development and Regulation Act, 1951 or employing plant and machinery in the process of value addition to the final product having a distinct name or character of use. The manufacturing enterprises (micro, small and medium)

were defined in term of investment in plant and machinery (Table 4.2).

Table 4.1: Components of the First Tranche

(₹ crore)

S. No.	Areas of focus	Amount
1.	Collateral-free automatic loans for businesses including micro, small and medium enterprises (MSMEs)	3,00,000
2.	Subordinate debt for stresses MSMEs	20,000
3.	Equity infusion through fund of funds	50,000
4.	Employees provident fund (EPF) support for business and workers for 3 months more (i.e. March, April and May)	2,800
5.	EPF contribution reduced for business and workers for 3 months	6,750
6.	Special liquidity scheme for non-banking financial companies (NBFCs), housing finance corporations (HFCs) and mutual fund institutions (MFIs)	30,000
7.	Partial credit guarantee scheme 2.0 for NBFCs	45,000
8.	Liquidity injection for power companies	90,000
9.	Liquidity through rate reduction of tax deduction at source (TDS)/tax collection at source (TCS)	50,000
10.	**Total size of the tranche**	**5,94,550**

2. **Service Enterprise:** Enterprises engaged in providing or rendering of services (micro, small and medium) were defined in terms of investment in equipment (Table 4.2).

From July 1, 2020, the distinction between manufacturing enterprises and service enterprises was abolished. Similarly, instead of a single investment criterion, a composite criterion (investment and turnover) was introduced. Thus,

1. An enterprise is defined as *micro* where the investment in plant and machinery or equipment does not exceed ₹ 1 crore and turnover does not exceed ₹ 5 crore.
2. An enterprise is defined as *small* where the investment in plant and machinery or equipment does not exceed ₹ 10 crore and turnover does not exceed ₹ 50 crore.

Table 4.2: Criteria for Classification of Micro, Small and Medium Enterprises under Micro, Small and Medium Enterprises Development Act, 2006

Prior to July 1, 2020		
	Enterprises	
	Manufacturing enterprises (investment in plant and machinery)	Service enterprises (investment in equipments)
Micro	Did not exceed ₹ 25 lakh	Did not exceed ₹ 10 lakh
Small	More than ₹ 25 lakh but did not exceed ₹ 5 crore	More than ₹ 10 lakh but did not exceed ₹ 2 crore
Medium	More than ₹ 5 crore but did not exceed ₹ 10 crore	More than ₹ 2 crore but did not exceed ₹ 5 crore
From July 1, 2020		
	Investment in plant and machinery or equipment	Turnover
Micro	Does not exceed ₹ 1 crore	Does not exceed ₹ 5 crore
Small	Does not exceed ₹ 10 crore	Does not exceed ₹ 50 crore
Medium	Does not exceed ₹ 50 crore	Does not exceed ₹ 250 crore

Source: Government of India, Ministry of Micro, Small and Medium Enterprises, Notification No. S.O. 1702 (E) dated June 1, 2020.

3. An enterprise is defined as *medium* where the investment in plant and machinery or equipment does not exceed ₹ 50 crore and turnover does not exceed ₹ 250 crore (Table 4.2).

4.2 Second Tranche for Poor and Middle Class

Announced on May 14, 2020, it was focused on the poor and lower middle class. It included rental housing facility for migrant workers, free foodgrains for those without ration cards and loan schemes for farmers and street vendors. Following were the elements of the second tranche:

1. Free foodgrains supply to migrants for 2 months. The measure was expected to benefit 8 crore migrants.
2. One nation, one ration card scheme for 67 crore beneficiaries in 23 states, covering 83 percent registered under public distribution scheme (PDS). The scheme will use Aadhaar to allow those entitled to access PDS to draw their quota from anywhere in the country.
3. Interest subsidy of ₹ 1,500 crore under Mudra Shishu loans.
4. Special credit facility of ₹ 5,000 crore for street vendors. The scheme is expected to help 50 lakh vendors.
5. ₹ 6,000 crore employment push for tribals by using funds under Compensatory Afforestation and Planning Authority (CAMPA).
6. Government to launch scheme under PM-Awas Yojana to provide homes at affordable rent to migrant labourers/urban poor.
7. Government-funded housing in cities to be converted into affordable rental housing complexes under public-private-partnership (PPP) mode.
8. ₹ 30,000 crore additional emergency working capital funding through National Bank for Agriculture and Rural Development (NABARD).
9. ₹ 2,00,000 crore concessional credit boost to 2.5 crore farmers through Kisan Credit Cards.
10. Government to extend credit-linked subsidy scheme for

middle income group (annual income ₹ 6 to ₹ 18 lakh) housing up to March 2021.

Table 4.3 presents the components and the amounts allocated under the second tranche.

Table 4.3: Components of the Second Tranche

(₹ crore)

S. No.	Areas of focus	Amount
1.	Free food to migrants	3,500
2.	Interest subvention on Mudra loans	1,500
3.	Credit line to street vendors	5,000
4.	Credit-linked subsidy scheme for housing	70,000
5.	Farmers refinance via NABARD	30,000
6.	CAMPA funds	6,000
7.	Kisan credit cards	2,00,000
8.	Total size of the tranche	3,16,000

4.3 Third Tranche for Farming Sector

On May 15, 2020, Government announced a mix of financial, legislative and other reform measures aimed largely at increasing the pricing power of farmers. Government proposed to dismantle historical domestic trade barriers to free food and commodities markets with a view to increase the share of farmers' profit in farm income. Government resolved to amend the Essential Commodities Act, 1955, make a central law on agriculture marketing and create a legal framework to provide price assurance to farmers and help improve the quality of their produce.

The tranche aggregated to ₹ 1.63 lakh crore, the details of which are given in Table 4.4.

4.4 Fourth Tranche for Privatization of the Economy

On May 16, 2020, Government announced the fourth set of measures which included a major opening up of coal, defence production, civil aviation, power, space, social infrastructure and atomic energy for private participation. The measures announced were intended to signal India's readiness to proactively seek investment and instil confidence in business circles.

Table 4.4: Components of the Third Tranche

(₹ crore)

S. No.	Areas of focus	Amount
1.	Financial facility for agricultural infrastructure projects	1,00,000
2.	Animal Husbandry Development Fund to support private investments in dairy processing, cattle feed infrastructure etc.	15,000
3.	Pradhan Mantri Matsya Sampada Yojana for fisheries to provide jobs to over 55 lakh and double exports to ₹ 1 lakh crore	20,000
4.	National Animal Disease Control Programme to prevent foot and mouth disease and to ensure 100 percent vaccination of cattle	13,343
5.	Scheme to help 2,00,000 micro food enterprises to meet FSSAI standards, build brand and market	10,000
6.	Scheme to employ 1 million hectare land for herbal cultivation in two years	4,000
7.	Subsidies currently available to TOP (tomatoes, onions and potatoes) to be extended to all fruits and vegetables	500
8.	Scheme to develop infrastructure related to beekeeping	500
9.	**Total size of the tranche**	**1,63,343**

Following were the main elements of the fourth tranche.

1. **Coal:** Government will immediately offer 50 coal mines for commercial mining by private sector without end-use restrictions. The mines will be auctioned on revenue-

sharing basis under a simplified regime to increase ease of doing business. Companies can bid even if they do not have experience in coal mining and can sell the output in the open market. Government also announced a ₹ 50,000 crore investment plan for creating infrastructure such as railway tracks and conveyors to evacuate coal from old and new mines.

Government had earlier approved the promulgation of Mineral Laws (Amendment) Ordinance, 2020 which allowed coal mining by any company present in sectors other than steel and power, and scrapped the captive end-use criterion. Now there is no distinction between captive and non-captive mines.

It may be recalled that in 2018, the Government had allowed commercial mining by private utilities. The Centre had set a mining target of 1.5 billion tonnes of coal by 2020. Of this, 1 billion tonne was to come from Coal India Limited (CIL) and 0.5 billion tonnes from non-CIL sources.

With above reforms in place, coal mining has been unshackled from the nationalisation of 1973 and the monopoly of public sector CIL ended. Prior to these reforms, only CIL was allowed to sell coal to end-users.

It is noteworthy that despite having the world's fourth largest coal reserves, India imports around 235 million tonnes of coal at huge cost in terms of foreign exchange. India's dependence on imports of coal will substantially reduce after these reform measures which have come at a time when global energy scenario is uncertain.

2. **Defence Production:**

- List of weapons/platforms to be notified for import ban. The list of weapons and platforms will be increasingly expanded to boost local manufacturing.
- Promoting indigenisation of spares which are currently imported.
- Corporatisation of ordnance factory board.

- Stock market listing.
- Foreign direct investment (FDI) limit in defence manufacturing raised from the present 49 percent to 74 percent under the automatic route.

3. **Civil Aviation:**

- Easing of restrictions on the use of Indian air space to increase efficiency of passenger aircrafts to save fuel and time. Currently, only 60 percent of domestic airspace is freely available.
- Six more airports to be bid out on public-private-partnership (PPP) basis in second round. Six more in third round.
- Additional investment by private players in 12 airports expected to be ₹ 13,000 crore.
- India to become global hub for maintenance, repair and overhaul.

4. **Power Sector:**

- Tariff policy reforms.
- Direct benefit transfer (DBT) for subsidy.
- Smart pre-paid metres.
- Time-bound grant of open access.
- Distribution companies (Discoms) to be penalised for load shedding.
- Electricity distribution utilities or power departments in the Union Territories (UTs) will be privatised for better service and efficiency.

5. **Space:** Private firms to be allowed in the field of satellites and other space-based services.

- Private sector to be allowed to use Indian Space Research Organization (ISRO) facilities.

6. **Social Infrastructure:** Government's share in viability gap funding for development of social infrastructure, including hospitals, raised from 20 percent to 30 percent, with a total outlay of ₹ 8,100 crore.
7. **Atomic Energy:** Research reactor to be set up in PPP mode for production of medical isotopes.

4.5 Fifth Tranche Focused on MGNREGS

On May 17, 2020, Government announced the fifth and the final tranche of policy reforms and fiscal incentives. The main focus was on Mahatma Gandhi National Rural Employment Guarantee Scheme (MGNREGS)—the flagship rural job guarantee scheme of the Central Government. In the budget for 2020-21, an allocation of ₹ 61,000 crore was made for the scheme. With millions of daily wagers and others returning to their villages in the wake of COVID-19 pandemic, there has been a surge in demand for work in rural areas. Hence, Government announced, as part of the fifth tranche, an additional allocation of ₹ 40,000 crore for MGNREGS. Original allocation and additional allocation make for ₹ 1,01,000 crore, making MGNREGS the only social welfare programme in the country with a kitty of ₹ 1,00,000 crore or more. MGNREGS has emerged as the backbone of rural income for the poor. It guarantees 100 days of work for one person in a year. The wage rate is ₹ 202 per day. There are demands to increase this limit to 150 days.

Other components of the fifth tranche were as under:

1. A substantial hike in the borrowing limit for states from 3 percent to 5 percent of gross state domestic product (GSDP) for the current fiscal year, subject to their carrying out specific reforms.
2. A new plan to end the monopoly of public sector enterprises (PSEs) and open up sectors for private participation. For the sake of public interest, a minimum of one and a maximum of four PSEs will continue to operate.
3. Substantial ease of compliance for businesses, including relaxations in the insolvency and bankruptcy framework.
4. Creation of a robust public health infrastructure covering districts and blocks.
5. Launch of a digital education programme.
6. Initiative for mental health and emotional well-being of teachers, students and families.

On May 17, 2020, Finance Minister said that the

Government has provided ₹ 11,02,650 crore stimulus in the five tranches. Earlier, stimulus worth ₹ 9,94,403 crore was infused in the system through fiscal policy measures that included ₹ 1,70,000 crore relief package on May 26 and ₹ 8,01,603 crore monetary measures by the RBI since March 27 (Table 4.5).

Table 4.5: Aatmanirbhar Package at a Glance

(₹ crore)

Scheme/Tranche	Date	Amount
Earlier measures, of which:	...	**9,94,403**
PM Garib Kalyan Yojana	March 26, 2020	1,70,000
Reserve Bank of India (RBI) monetary measures	March-April 2020	8.01,603
Five tranches	May 13 to 17, 2020	**11,02,650**
Grand total		**20,97,053**

4.6 Assessment of Aatmanirbhar Bharat Package

Various relief and reform measures announced by the Government were hailed as radical and historic by economists. They were as structural in nature as the ones announced in the early 1990s. The then Government led by Prime Minister Narsimha Rao forced to liberalize and open up the Indian economy in the face of acute balance of payment crisis.

In the present case, the stimulus for reforms to *unshackle* the economy was provided by the crisis created by Covid pandemic. In fact, the Government seized the crisis to push forward long-pending industrial and other economic reforms in an atmosphere of least political resistance.

Whatever may have been the circumstances leading to these drastic reforms, they were steps in the right direction considering the changed and changing global realities. Post-Covid, uncertainty is reigning supreme and countries are thinking of self-sufficiency. World economies are unsure as to what extent they can depend on others in the future. Global firms are reducing their presence in China and relocating to other countries, shifting the supply chain in the process. The world is not going to be the same. The working environment (e.g. working from home) will change and so also the inter-personal contacts for business.

As in the case of announcing lockdowns, India is quite early to have taken the cue of self-sufficiency.

5

Favourable Factors for Indian Economy to Rebound

COVID-19 has devastated countries (including India) around the world in terms of human and economic loss. Although every covid-related casualty is regrettable, data suggest that India's performance to contain the pandemic is remarkable when compared with the situation in US, France, Britain, Italy, Spain, Germany and other European countries.

Why has India performed so well to cope with the deadly pandemic? The first and the foremost reason is the timely and effective action taken the Central and State Governments to implement the country-wide lockdown.

In spite of massive economic loss due to lockdown, India can look forward to revival of the economy in the near future. There are silver linings in the dark clouds.

5.1 The Resilient Agricultural Sector

When countrywide lockdown was announced from March 25, 2020, most of the economic activities came to a grinding halt in urban areas. However, rural India continued to be normal in view of the exemption from restrictions allowed to farmers to conduct farming operations, including harvesting and transporting their produce to grain markets with the general conditions of face covering, hand hygiene and social distancing. These exemptions helped to maintain continuity in supply chain, especially in view of harvesting and sowing season. Food Corporation of India and State Governments carried out massive procurement of *rabi* crops, mainly wheat.

India's foodgrains production was 285 million tonnes (MT) in 2018-19 which rose to record level of 295 MT in

2019-20. The target for 2020-21 has been set at 298 MT.

For details, see chapter 6 of this book.

5.2 Low Crude Oil Prices

At the beginning of 2020, global oil market was experiencing high oil output as a result of production increases in US, Canada, and some other non-OPEC+ countries. With Covid-19 outbreak in China, and the lockdown of Wuhan, a major industrial hub, oil prices tumbled down from US$ 68 per barrel in early January 2020 to US$ 53 per barrel in early February.

In mid-March 2020, Saudi Arabia announced it would pump a record 12.3 million barrel per day (mbpd), unleashing the so-called price war with Russia. The explosion of supply came as governments worldwide announced lockouts, crushing fuel demand.

As the outbreak grew into a pandemic, countries around the world were affected, causing panic and unplanned lockouts. Industries were shut down and transport and travel activities came to a screeching halt. This led to fall in oil prices and price war (in the form of discounts) among major oil exporters.

Oil prices started hovering around US$ 20 per barrel, causing immense harm to oil-dependent countries of Persian Gulf.

With 80 percent dependence on imports to meet domestic oil requirements, any reduction in international crude oil prices proves a windfall for India. Import bill comes down, making current account deficit in the balance of payments more manageable.

For details, see chapter 7 of this book.

5.3 China's Loss Can be India's Gain

The current world hostility towards China, the epicentre of coronavirus, can be converted into opportunity for India. Post-Covid, US-China trade war is likely to accelerate. On April 29,

2020, President Trump hinted at the possibility of US claiming damages from China for latter's mishandling of the coronavirus outbreak. It is claimed that the coronavirus originated in a laboratory in Wuhan and China failed to stop it at the source. Developed world, led by Australia, is demanding international probe for the causes of virus spread, which China is vehemently trying to stonewall.

In such a scenario, economic and financial distancing from China may be a policy prescription not only for US and its Western allies but also for other countries including India.

US and Western companies, at the behest of their governments, are planning to shift their manufacturing units and withdraw investment from China.

The COVID-19 pandemic has led several companies towards a realisation that de-coupling their supply chains from China may be necessary to mitigate risk arising out of natural and geopolitical disturbances.

India can be their next destination, provided we ready ourselves to milk the opportunity. This requires government incentives, Centre-States co-ordination, and joint venture offers from Indian corporates.

Although India has jumped on the ease-of-doing-business rank in recent years, it is yet to break into the top 50 countries.

In the recent past, most companies which withdrew from China preferred Taiwan, Thailand and Vietnam for re-location. Very few opted for India. It underscores the need to make India more business-friendly for prospective foreign investors.

For example, India can be an attractive hub for drugs at a time when China faces hostility, distrust and quality issues. Presently, China controls 55 percent of API, a key raw material for drug manufacturers, market in the world. On March 21, 2020, Union Cabinet approved a ₹ 10,000 crore incentive-based scheme to promote domestic manufacturing of APIs by setting up bulk drug parks.

India can also leverage the current anti-China feelings to push its exports globally in markets likely to be vacated by China.

5.4 Strong Diversified Manufacturing Base

India has established a strong and diversified manufacturing base for the production of a wide variety of basic and capital goods to meet the requirements of various sectors including heavy electrical, power generation and transmission industries, process equipment, automobiles, ships, aircrafts, mining, chemicals, petroleum etc. However, share of manufacturing sector in India's economy is still quite low. There is a considerable potential for growth which, in a globalized world economy, has to be based on improving productivity and competitiveness. Innovation and adoption of new technologies are the key factors in competitiveness. In the Indian context, opening of the economy and consequently the entry of international players has substantially enhanced the need for production of goods and services matching international standards. Indian industry has undertaken a number of steps to meet the needs of the customers in a fast changing environment.

5.5 Demographic Dividend

Presently, India is one of the youngest nations in the world with more than 62 percent of its population in the working age group (15-59 years), and more than 54 percent of its total population below 25 years of age. Its population pyramid is expected to bulge across the 15-59 age group over the next decade. It is further estimated that the average age of the population in India by 2020 will be 29 years as against 40 years in USA, 46 years in Europe and 47 years in Japan. In fact, during the next 20 years the labour force in the industrialized world is expected to decline by 4 percent, while in India it will increase by 32 percent. This poses a formidable challenge and a huge opportunity. To reap this demographic dividend which is expected to last for next 25 years, India needs to equip its workforce with employable skills and knowledge so that they can contribute substantively to the economic growth of the country.

India is midway through its demographic dividend—a period of time when demography gives economic growth a boost by expanding the working-age share of the population. To exploit this dividend and meet the growing aspirations of those entering the labour force, India's economy needs to create enough *good jobs*—jobs that are safe and pay well, and encourage firms and workers to improve skills and productivity.

If the massive population of India is properly educated and trained, it can prove a boon for the national economy. India's demographic dividend is essentially due to two factors: (a) declining birth rates, and (b) improvement in life expectancy. The declining birth rate changes the age distribution and makes for a smaller proportion of population in the dependent ages and for relatively larger share in the productive labour force. The result is low dependency ratio which can provide comparative cost advantage and competitiveness to the economy. Moreover, the global economy is expected to witness a skilled man power shortage to the extent of around 56 million by 2020. Thus, the *demographic dividend* in India needs to be exploited not only to expand the production possibility frontier but also to meet the skilled manpower requirements of India and other countries. [1]

Thus, in the longer run, there is another important potential strength arising from India's demographic trends. Dependency rate (ratio of dependent to working age population) is falling whereas that of industrialised countries and even China is rising. The presence of a skilled young population in an environment where investment is expanding and the industrial world ageing could be a major advantage. It is, however, important to realise that demographic dividend can be reaped only if there is massive investment in human resources development and skill formation and creation of an economic environment capable of absorbing relatively young working population in productive employment.

This demographic dividend can add to growth potential, provided three conditions are fulfilled.

1. Higher levels of health, education and skill development must be achieved.
2. An environment must be created in which the economy not only grows rapidly, but also enhances good quality employment/livelihood opportunities to meet the needs and aspirations of the youth.
3. Current size of the population is stabilized at the earliest.

Further growth of population as predicted will lead to overcrowding, poverty, under-nutrition, environmental deterioration, poor quality of life and increase in disease burden.

Prime Minister Narendra Modi, in his first Independent Day speech in his second term in office, raised the issue of uncontrolled population growth and its consequences for the country. Expressing his concerns on challenges that the growing population may pose, he said, "Today, from the ramparts of the Red Fort, I want to address the issue of population explosion in the country. Parents in India now need to give a serious thought to whether they will be able to fulfil their child's dreams and aspirations and support a new life. We cannot think of an unhealthy society, we cannot think of an uneducated society. In 21st century India, the ability to fulfil dreams starts with a person, starts with a family. If the population is not educated, not healthy, then neither the home nor the country can be happy. If the population is educated, empowered, and skilled and has adequate means available to achieve the right ambience to fulfil their wishes and needs, then I think the country can fulfil these things".

He further said, "Population explosion in the country will create various problems for the coming generations. Those who follow the policy of small family also contribute to the development of the nation, it is also a form of patriotism".

5.6 Preferred Destination for Investment

In the wake of economic liberalisation policy initiated in 1991, the Government of India has taken several measures to encourage foreign investment, both direct and portfolio, in almost all sectors of the economy. However, the emphasis has been on foreign direct investment (FDI) inflows in the: (a) development of infrastructure, (b) technological upgradation of Indian industry, (c) projects having the potential for creating employment opportunities on a large scale, and (d) setting up special economic zones and establishing manufacturing units therein. With a vast reservoir of skilled and cost-effective manpower, India is now recognized as one of the most attractive investment destinations by reputed international rating organisations.

Promotion of foreign direct investment forms an integral part of India's economic policies. The role of foreign direct investment in accelerating economic growth is by way of infusion of capital, technology and modern management practices. Government has put in place a liberal and transparent foreign investment regime where most activities are opened to foreign investment on automatic route without any limit on the extent of foreign ownership.

FDI, being a non-debt capital flow, is a leading source of external financing, especially for the developing economies. It not only brings in capital and technical know-how but also increases the competitiveness of the economy. Overall, it supplements domestic investment, much required for sustaining the high growth rate of the country. In recent years, significant changes have been made in the FDI policy regime by the Government to ensure that India becomes an increasingly attractive and investor-friendly destination.

Over the past few years, India has become an attractive destination for foreign investment owing, among other factors, to its large and rapidly growing consumer market, a developed commercial banking network, availability of skilled manpower and a package of fiscal incentives for foreign investors. The top investing countries in India include Mauritius, US, Japan, UK and Netherlands. The most important sectors attracting foreign investment are electrical equipment including computer software, transportation industry, telecommunications, and fuels.

India continues to retain its position as a preferred destination for investments. In her speech to the Parliament while presenting the Budget for 2019-20 (Final) on July 5, 2019, Finance Minister Nirmala Sitharaman remarked, "FDI inflows into India have remained robust despite global headwinds. Global Foreign Direct Investment (FDI) flows slid by 13 percent in 2018, to US$ 1.3 trillion from US$ 1.5 trillion the previous year—the third consecutive annual decline, according to UNCTAD's World Investment Report, 2019. India's FDI inflows in 2018-19 remained strong at US$ 64.375 billion marking a 6 percent growth over the previous year". [2]

Among the top sectors attracting FDI equity inflows, services, automobiles and chemicals were the major categories. This pick-up indicates the improvement in confidence of the foreign investors in the Indian economy.

To help revive economic activity by attracting more foreign direct investment (FDI), the Union Cabinet on August 28, 2019, relaxed several rules in areas such as single-brand retail, contract manufacturing, coal mining and digital media. 100 percent FDI in all coal sector activities was permitted and 26 percent FDI in digital media was allowed.

5.7 IT and IT-enabled Services

Government policy that favours innovation can have significant impact on growth and job creation in the economy. Furthermore, India has a latent science and engineering talent pool, which may be particularly advantageous. This strength should be capitalised to generate indigenous intellectual capital.

Telecommunications and IT are the twin sectors that best epitomize what modern, resurgent and young India is capable of accomplishing. Achievements in the recent past in the IT and telecom sectors are spectacular and unprecedented in India's history. Yet, it is the future that holds even more breathtaking possibilities. A fascinating opportunity has now arisen that rests on the foundations of what has been achieved in recent years in IT and telecom. IT and IT-enabled services have the potential to script India's future across the economy, society and government.

IT has been contributing substantially to the economic growth of the country. More importantly, it can immensely help in accelerating the growth momentum by enhancing efficiency, competitiveness and technological edge across sectors, including particularly strategic sectors. Equally significant is the contribution of IT in enabling inclusive growth and development, and in ensuring that people across the length and breadth of the country have access to the opportunities generated by growth.

Differential access to economic opportunities across nations that characterized the past has been fundamentally impacted and altered by IT and telecom. The same phenomenon can be exploited to help equalize access to opportunity within the country, straddling urban and rural, rich and poor. Ubiquitous and reliable connectivity holds the key. IT is thus not just a major part of a better future, but more importantly, is the key instrument in realising it. Imagining a credibly optimistic future and designing IT policy to realize that vision, could therefore be a self-fulfilling prophesy.

India is today a global source of skilled IT manpower. IT permeates all aspects of society, business, governance, finance and indeed every other aspect of modern life. Hence, India's strengths in IT constitute a major strategic advantage that needs to be maintained and systematically nurtured. Existing capabilities are already powerful enough to transform the economy, government and society.

Concerns about cyber security in general and security of telecom infrastructure in particular are escalating. Current efforts in these areas need to be stepped up by appropriate arrangements for co-ordination across multiple agencies involved, if they are to be effective in meeting new and emerging challenges.

5.8 India Recognized as Economic Powerhouse

Beginning 21st century, India has become an economic power to be reckoned with. On June 2, 2020, US President

Donald Trump called for the expansion of G-7 to include Russia, South Korea, Australia and India. It may be recalled that 2019 G-7 Summit, held in Southern France, was attended by Prime Minister Narendra Modi, as a special guest of French President Emmanuel Macron.

G-7 grouping is an assemblage of the world's largest economies and currently includes Canada, France, United Kingdom, Italy, Japan, Germany and the United States.

US President Trump's call for the inclusion of India is an acknowledgement of the markedly changed economic and geopolitical environment witnessed presently.

If G-7 becomes G-11, India will be the fourth largest economy (after US, Japan and Germany) of the new grouping.

With India's economy also reeling from the effects of the pandemic, the government has introduced a series of measures geared towards making India a lucrative and safe proposition for foreign investors. India's inclusion in the proposed G-11 would go a long way towards solidifying India's commitment to fashioning itself as a key manufacturing destination in the coming years.

5.9 Burgeoning Foreign Exchange Reserves

India's comfortable foreign exchange reserves (US$ 500 billion, the highest ever) provide confidence in the country's ability to manage balance of payments. These reserves indicate an import cover of about 1 year against the IMF's benchmark of 3 months. Foreign exchange reserves act as the first line of defence for India in case of economic emergency. These reserves facilitate external trade and payment and promote orderly development and maintenance of foreign exchange market. It may be recalled that India's foreign exchange reserves had dipped to as low as US$ 1 billion in early 1991 which prompted the then Prime Minister Narsimha Rao to introduce economic reforms in India.

5.10 Summary of Strengths of the Indian Economy

In addressing the current slowdown, India has several

advantages and comforting factors including the following:

1. **High Share of Services in GDP:** India has a relatively high share of services in GDP (around 54-55 percent) than many other developing countries. Historically, across countries, services tend to be less affected by cyclical downturns than manufacturing. This factor is likely to moderate the negative effect on overall GDP growth.
2. **Vibrant Agricultural Sector:** With industrial sector showing signs of slowdown, a vibrant agricultural sector is a silver lining in the otherwise gloomy scenario. The share of agriculture in gross domestic product (GDP), which has been declining for quite some time and hovers around 14-15 percent, is likely to increase.
3. **Expanding Rural Market:** Rural income and consumption are strong and likely to remain so in view of implementation of following policy measures:

- Mahatma Gandhi National Rural Employment Guarantee Scheme (MGNREGS).
- Remunerative minimum support prices (MSPs) for various crops.
- Doubling Farmers Income by 2022-23.
- Pradhan Mantri Kisan SAMPADA Yojana.
- Pradhan Mantri Kisan Samman Nidhi (PM-KISAN).
- Pradhan Mantri Fasal Bima Yojana (PMFBY).
- Pradhan Mantri Krishi Sinchai Yojana (PMKSY).
- Pradhan Mantri Kisan Maandhan Yojana (PMKMY).

4. **Infrastructure and Logistics Development:** The ambitious programme of infrastructure investment under public-private-partnership mode provides the basis for offsetting slowdown in corporate investment in manufacturing.
5. **Fiscal Deficit:** In view of lack of overall demand, Government enjoys considerable leverage in terms of magnitude of fiscal deficit.
6. **Robust Financial System:** India's financial institutions, particularly banks, and financial markets have continued to

function normally during successive nationwide lockdowns.

7. **Lower Rate of Inflation:** India has maintained its macroeconomic stability by containing inflation within the comfortable zone of 3.5 to 4.5 percent.
8. **Social Security Net:** India has a robust and digitally managed social security net to look after the needs of vulnerable and disadvantaged sections of the society.
9. **Realistic Exchange Rate Policy:** The distinct improvement in the external sector in India has enabled a progressive liberalization of the exchange and payments regime. The exchange rate is market-determined. Exchange rate management is flexible without fixed or pre-announced targets or bands, with interventions primarily to ensure orderly market conditions. India's exchange rate policy is perceived to be realistic and the exchange rate is among the least volatile in emerging market economies.
10. **Non-economic Factors:** Political stability is an asset for India. Political stability of a country is an important driver of technological advancement. With respect to financing technological development, in politically stable economies the availability of funds and venture capital is attainable irrespective of the size of the firms with respect to people employed. In contrast, in economies that are high in political instability, financing is more challenging especially for small size firms.

India's growth story at a fast pace is likely to continue because of its strong macro fundamentals. Over the years, India has built an extensive network of social security programmes and schemes including the flagship Mahatma Gandhi National Rural Employment Guarantee Scheme (MGNREGS). These uniquely Indian versions of automatic stabilizers should protect the poor from the extreme impact of the slowdown.

Compared to other developing economies, India has several strengths that can help mitigate the adverse effects of slowdown. The Government has taken several measures in this direction and the economy is expected to return to the high growth trajectory. Sustained interest in India as a long-term investment destination and a comfortable reserve position suggest that the external sector can continue to support stability and growth. As the monetary and fiscal stimuli work their way through, and if calm and confidence are restored in the global markets, India can see economic turnaround.

This belief that Indian economy will rebound is strengthened in view of the resilience shown by the Indian economy in recent years. For example, Indian economy escaped almost unscathed during the unprecedented financial crisis of 2007-08 when economies of developed countries went topsy-turvy. Financial giants, including Lehman Brothers, collapsed like house of cards.

The entrepreneurial culture in India is picking up. Bangalore has been listed within the world's 20 leading start-up cities in the 2015 Start-up Genome Project ranking. It is also ranked as one of the world's five fastest growing start-up cities. Nevertheless, much of this entrepreneurship is limited to IT. To create new jobs, India must move beyond its reliance on IT achievements and the industrial conglomerates that drove earlier post-liberalization growth. For example, India needs to develop technological capabilities to serve the requirements of its core industries—capital goods used in manufacturing industries are mostly imported, as are electronic goods.

There is tremendous scope to boost entrepreneurship in India. Some sectors immediately provide opportunities for growth. For example, the auto components sector is expected to see substantial growth. Sectors like IT infrastructure, biotechnology, healthcare and education, too are poised to grow several times in size over the next couple of years.

Members of the global economy, including businesses and foreign governments, have started taking note of India's rise and recognizing opportunities for investments and enterprise. India's massive workforce and democratic functioning suggest that the future of labour-intensive industry lies here. Undoubtedly, India is poised to claim its rightful place as world economic power in the 21st century, being referred to as the Asian Century.

At Independence, India had all the ills of a politically, socially and economically ravaged country. Agriculture was at subsistence level, which led in subsequent years to imports of foodgrains. Industry, except for sundry textile mills and a steel plant or two was almost non-existent. And the infrastructure was skeletal, confined to ports, roads, and railway lines laid mainly to meet a colonial regime's needs. The other inheritance was an administration more oriented towards maintenance of law and order than economic and social development.

73 years is an insignificant period in the history of an ancient land like India. However, when viewed from the angle of social, political and economic development, these 73 years have been the most remarkable in its life, as they have witnessed a backward, colonially-oppressed country transformed into an economically vibrant, modern nation set to take its place among the advanced nations of the world.

As a result of development efforts since Independence in 1947, India has emerged as a nation which can claim to have a strong agricultural, industrial, trade and economic foundation and an administration wholly tuned towards achieving rapid development.

In short, fundamental of the Indian economy are strong. Retail inflation rate is under control. Fiscal deficit is also under control. Foreign exchange reserves at around US$ 490 billion are robust.

Endnotes

1. Population growth and its relation to economic growth has been a matter of debate for a long time. The early Malthusian view was that population growth is likely to impede economic growth because it will put pressure on the available resources, result in reduction in per capita income and resources. This, in turn, will result in deterioration in quality of life. Contrary to the Malthusian predictions, several of the East Asian countries have

been able to achieve economic prosperity and improvement in quality of life in spite of population growth. This has been attributed to the increase in productivity due to development and utilization of innovative technologies by the young educated population who formed the majority of the growing population. These countries have been able to exploit the dynamics of demographic transition to achieve economic growth by using the human resources as the engine driving the economic development. Improved employment with adequate emoluments has promoted saving and investment which, in turn, stimulated economic growth.

2. Government of India, Ministry of Finance, Budget Papers 2019-20 (Final), *Speech of Minister of Finance*, July 5, 2019, para 36.

6

Robust and Resilient Agricultural Sector

6.1 Why is Agricultural Sector Important for India?

Agricultural sector occupies a key position in the Indian economy. Agriculture (inclusive of animal husbandry, forestry and fishing) is central to the nutrition needs of India and also remains the largest sector of India's economy as a source of employment. According to the Fifth Annual Employment-Unemployment Survey of the Ministry Labour and Employment, 45.7 percent of India's workforce in 2014-15 was employed in agriculture. Around 13 to 14 percent of India's national income originates from the agricultural sector. It is imperative that the problems of farmers are addressed with a sense of urgency. Agriculture being a State subject, the bulk of public investment in agriculture takes place at the level of States and the Central Government supports the States as a catalyst.

Agricultural products like cereals (mainly rice), tea, coffee, cashew, spices, tobacco and leather are important items of India's exports and hence foreign exchange earnings. Agriculture is also the source of raw material for agro-based industries including textiles, cigarettes, jute, sugar, paper, processed foodstuffs and *vanaspati*.

Moreover, agricultural sector provides market for capital goods (tractors, pump sets and other agricultural machinery), inputs (fertilisers, insecticides), and light consumer goods. The nation has invested huge resources for the development of agriculture under various plans.

The development of the agricultural sector depends, to a large extent, on such core industries as power, petroleum, fertilisers and machine tools. Thus, there is inter-dependence between agriculture and industry.

Agriculture being a state subject, the primary responsibility for increasing agriculture production, enhancing productivity, and exploring the vast untapped potential of the sector rests with the State Governments. However, in order to supplement the efforts of the State Governments, a number of Centrally-sponsored and Central Sector schemes are being implemented for enhancing agricultural production and productivity in the country and increasing the income of the farming community.

6.2 Components of Agriculture and Allied Sectors

India is the land of diverse agro-ecologies. It produces a number of major and minor agricultural commodities.

There are two main agricultural seasons in India: (a) *kharif* under which crops are planted at the onset of the Southwest monsoon in June-July and harvested in September-October and (b) *rabi* under which crops are planted usually between October and December and harvested between March and May. Major *kharif* crops are rice, jowar, bajra, maize, cotton, sugarcane, soyabean and groundnut. Major *rabi* crops are wheat, barley, gram, linseed, rapeseed and mustard.

Due to its diverse climatic, soil and terrain conditions, a wide variety of crops are grown in different parts of the country. The cropping pattern in India is influenced by a host of factors. Cropping pattern refers to the distribution of cultivated land among different crops grown in a country. Cropping pattern reveals the nature of agricultural operations, e.g. the importance of food crops vis-à-vis cash crops. Cropping pattern is influenced by a host of factors which can be broadly classified into two categories: (a) physical factors and (b) economic factors.

There has been no significant change in the cropping pattern during the post-Independence period. The present cropping pattern is unbalanced as it is heavily tilted in favour of paddy and wheat while area under oilseeds and pulses is less than required.

Among the physical factors, the important ones are soil conditions, extent of rainfall and type of climate. The economic factors include relative prices of agricultural commodities, size of the farms, availability of inputs, demand conditions, system of land holding and government policy regarding exports, imports, taxes and subsidies.

Agriculture and allied sectors in India consist of the following 4 sub-sectors: (a) crop sector, (b) livestock, (c) fisheries and (d) forestry.

6.2.1 Crop Sector: Being the largest sector in agriculture, crop sector holds a large number of contributors, viz. field crops, plantation crops and horticultural crops. This sector constitutes the backbone of the India's food economy.

A. Field Crops: These include the following:

1. Cereals (paddy, wheat, barley, maize, gram and other cereals).
2. Pulses (gram, blackgram, moth, other pulses).
3. Oilseeds (linseed, sesame, groundnut, mustard, soyabean, sunflower, rapeseed).
4. Fibres (cotton, jute, mesta and others).
5. Sugarcane.

B. Plantation Crops: These include the following:

1. Tea, coffee, tobacco, opium, betel leaves, saffron, cocoa, rubber, coconut, cashew.
2. Condiments and spices (cardamom, chillies, black pepper, turmeric, cumin, fenugreek, tamarind, cloves, nutmeg). Some of these crops constitute important items of India's exports. India is the largest producer, processor, consumer and exporter of cashew in the world. Coconut is an important tree crop grown extensively in coastal areas providing livelihood to about 10 million people in cultivation, processing and related activities.

C. Horticultural Crops: These consist of the following:

1. Fruits (banana, mango, grapes, papaya, apple, orange and others).
2. Vegetables (potato, onion, tomato, radish, carrot, green

peas, and others).

6.2.2 Livestock: It consists of the following: (a) milk, meat, eggs, (b) wool and hair, (c) silkworm and honey cocoon and (d) dung.

6.2.3 Fisheries: It comprises: (a) inland fish and (b) marine fish.

6.2.4 Forestry: This sector is composed of: (a) industrial wood, (b) firewood and (c) non-timber forest products.

Accelerating the growth rate of agricultural production is seen as central to a more inclusive growth. The Government of India has launched a series of programmes and schemes in recent years to rejuvenate agriculture and improve farm income.

6.3 COVID-19 and Agricultural Sector

When countrywide lockdown was announced from March 25, 2020, most of the economic activities came to a grinding halt in urban areas. However, rural India continued to be normal in view of the exemption from restrictions allowed to farmers to conduct farming operations, including harvesting and transporting their produce to grain markets with the general conditions of face covering, hand hygiene and social distancing. These exemptions helped to maintain continuity in supply chain, especially in view of harvesting and sowing season. Food Corporation of India and State Governments carried out massive procurement of *rabi* crops, mainly wheat.

India's foodgrains production was 285 million tonnes (MT) in 2018-19 which rose to record level of 295 MT in 2019-20. The target for 2020-21 has been set at 299 MT.

With industrial and services sectors showing signs of slowdown, a vibrant agricultural sector is a silver lining in the otherwise gloomy scenario. The share of agriculture in gross domestic product (GDP), which has been declining for quite some time and hovers around 14-15 percent, is likely to increase.

6.3.1 Normal Monsoon and Record Foodgrains Production for 2020-21: On April 15, 2020, India Meteorological Department (IMD) predicted normal rainfall over India during south-west monsoon season (June to September), with an error margin of ± 5 percent. Based on this, it has been estimated that India will harvest a record output of 299 million tonnes of foodgrains during the 2020-21 agricultural season.

It may be recalled that soon after Independence in 1947 and partition of the country, India suffered heavy deficits in the availability of foodgrains. In 1950-51, total fodgrains production was 50 million tonnes. Over the last 73 years, it has increased almost six-fold. Population has increased around three and a half-fold: from 36 crore in 1951 to 130 crore presently. Thus, the per capita availability of foodgrains has substantially improved and the country is well-placed in terms of basic necessity.

Not only cultivation, but agriculture-related activities—plantation, horticulture, cattle breeding, fishing, poultry farming, dairy farming—have also remained, by and large, immune to Covid crisis and their future growth is assured.

India is a highly diversified and self-sufficient economy. This is in sharp contrast to single-commodity (crude oil) economies of Middle-East and Persian Gulf where almost all goods and services are imported except oil.

6.4 Doubling Farmers Income by 2022-23

While talking about income of the farmers at a Kisan Rally in Bareilly (Uttar Pradesh) on February 28, 2016, the Prime Minister stated that it is his dream to see farmers double their income by 2022, when the country completes 75 years of its Independence. It is obvious that he was referring to double the current income of the farmers or income for the agricultural year 2015-16 by agricultural year 2022-23, i.e. 7 years away from the base year 2015-16.

Farmers make up nearly half of India's workforce.

Therefore, for India to flourish, its farmers and the farm economy must prosper. It is against this background that the Prime Minister has called for doubling farmers' incomes by 2022. To achieve this goal, a strong programme for agricultural transformation is required. It should include numerous measures to raise farm productivity, bring remunerative prices to farmers, put farmers' land to productive uses when they are not able to farm it themselves and improve the implementation of relief measures.

Enhancing agricultural productivity requires efficient use of inputs, introduction of new technologies and shifting from low to high value commodities. It needs to expand the scope of irrigation to increase crop intensity, improve access to irrigation, enhance the seed replacement rate and encourage the balanced use of fertilizers. Precision farming and related new technologies, that allow highly efficient farming and conserve resources, must be spread through appropriate policy interventions. Conditions conducive to shift into high value commodities such as horticulture, dairying, poultry, piggery, small ruminant husbandry, fisheries and forestry need to be created.

Unsurprisingly, the Prime Minister has set the goal of doubling farmers' income by 2022-23 over that in 2015-16. Achieving this goal would require significantly faster growth in nearly all variables that positively impact farmers' incomes.

6.5 Direct Benefit Transfer (DBT) in Fertiliser Sector

Government of India introduced DBT system for fertilizer subsidy on pilot basis with effect from October 2016. Under the fertilizer DBT system, 100 percent subsidy on various fertilizer grades is released to the fertilizer companies on the basis of actual sales made by the retailers to the beneficiaries. The sale of all subsidized fertilizers to farmers/buyers is made through point-of-sale (PoS) devices installed at each retail shop and the beneficiaries are identified through Aadhaar card, kisan credit card (KCC), voter identity card etc. The implementation of the DBT scheme requires development of PoS devices at every retail shop, training of retailers for using PoS device, stock initialization in the PoS device after verifying the physical stock at retail point, before making sales transactions. Presently, the DBT scheme is under implementation in 17 pilot districts. Based on the deployment of PoS devices in different States, the Department of Fertilizers will extend the DBT scheme to other States in a phased manner.

The benefits of the DBT scheme are as under:

1. DBT framework is a beneficiary-driven subsidy payment mechanism at national level.
2. It creates Aadhaar-seeded data base of beneficiaries and provides transaction visibility at the level of buyers.
3. By linking the actual sales to subsidy payments, it facilitates a more transparent and faster tracking of funds along the value chain, i.e. from manufacturers to beneficiaries.
4. Diversion of fertilizers is expected to be minimized.

6.6 Remunerative Minimum Support Prices (MSPs)

An important element of the agricultural price policy of the Government of India is the announcement every year of MSPs for major commodities. The co-operative societies and government agencies have helped the farmers to escape the exploitative practices of the private traders.

Assurance of a remunerative and stable price environment is considered very important for increasing agricultural production and productivity since the market place for agricultural produce tends to be inherently unstable, which often inflicts undue losses on the growers, even when they adopt the best available technology package and produce efficiently. Towards this end, MSPs for major agricultural products are fixed by the Government, each year, after taking into account the cost of inputs.

Policy of the Government regarding MSPs was enunciated

by the Finance Minister Arun Jaitley in his budget speech to the Parliament on February 1, 2018. He said, "...in our party's manifesto it has been stated that the farmers should realize at least 50 percent more than the cost of their produce, in other words, one and a half times of the cost of their production. Government has been very much sensitive to this resolutions and it has declared minimum support price (MSP) for the majority of rabi crops at least at one and a half times the cost involved. Now, we have decided to implement this resolution as a principle for the rest of crops". [1]

On June 1, 2020, Central Government announced higher MSPs for 14 kharif (summer sown) crops for 2020-21. The support price for the most popular kharif crop paddy was increased from ₹ 1,815 per quintal to ₹ 1,868 per quintal.

6.7 Pradhan Mantri Fasal Bima Yojana (PMFBY)

Prime Minister Narendra Modi unveiled the new scheme Pradhan Mantri Fasal Bima Yojana (PMFBY) on January 13, 2016. This scheme will help in decreasing the burden of premiums on farmers who take loans for their cultivation and will also safeguard them against the inclement weather.

It has also been decided to make the settlement process of the insurance claim, fast and easy so that the farmers do not face any trouble regarding the crop insurance plan. This scheme will be implemented in every state of India, in association with respective State Governments. The scheme will be administered under the Ministry of Agriculture and Farmers Welfare, Government of India.

6.7.1 Objectives of the Scheme: These are as under:

1. To provide insurance coverage and financial support to the farmers in the event of failure of any of the notified crop as a result of natural calamities, pests and diseases.
2. To stabiles the income of farmers to ensure their continuous process in farming.
3. To encourage farmers to adopt innovative and modern

agricultural practices.

4. To ensure flow of credit to the agriculture sector.

6.7.2 Highlight of the Scheme:

1. There will be a uniform premium of only 2 percent to be paid by farmers for all Kharif crops and 1.5 percent for all Rabi crops. In case of annual commercial and horticultural crops, the premium to be paid will be only 5 percent.
2. The premium rates to be paid by farmers are very low and balance premium will be paid by the Government to provide full insured amount to the farmers against crop loss in any natural calamities.
3. There is no upper limit on Government subsidy. Even if balance premium is 90 percent, it will be borne by the Government.
4. Earlier, there was a provision of capping the premium rate which is low claims being paid to farmers. Now this is removed and farmers will get claim against full sum insured without any reduction.
5. The use of technology will be encouraged to a great extent. Smart phones, Remote sensing drone and GPS technologies will be used to capture and upload data of crop cutting to reduce the delays in the claim payment.
6. The insurance plan will be handled under a single insurance company, Agriculture Insurance Company of India (AIC).

PMFBY is a replacement scheme of National Agriculture Insurance Scheme (NAIS) and Modified National Agriculture Insurance Scheme (MNAIS) and hence exempted from the service tax.

Moreover, District Level Monitoring Committee (DLMC) already overseeing the implementation & monitoring of the ongoing crop insurance schemes like National Agricultural Insurance Scheme (NAIS), Weather Based Crop Insurance Scheme (WBCIS), Modified National Agricultural Insurance Scheme (MNAIS) and Coconut Palm Insurance Scheme (CPIS) shall be responsible for proper management of the Scheme.

Regarding PMFBY, the Finance Minister Arun Jaitley in his 2017-18 Budget Speech on February 1 observed, "At the time of sowing, farmers should feel secure against natural calamities. The *Fasal Bima Yojana* launched by our Government is a major step in this direction. The coverage of this scheme will be increased from 30 percent of cropped area in 2016-17 to 40 percent in 2017-18 and 50 percent in 2018-19. The Budget provision of ₹ 5,500 crore for this Yojana in 2016-17 (budget estimates) was increased to ₹ 13,240 crore in 2016-17 (revised estimates) to settle the arrear claims. For 2017-18, I have provided a sum of ₹ 9,000 crore. The sum insured under this Yojana has more than doubled from ₹ 69,000 crore in Kharif 2015 to ₹ 1,41,625 crore in Kharif 2016". [2]

Commenting on the *Fasal Bima Yojana,* NITI Aayog has stated, "Natural disasters such as droughts, floods, cyclones, storms, landslides and earthquakes can lead to extreme distress and hardship among many small farmers who lead a subsistence existence. In these situations, they need at least a minimal amount of relief at a rapid pace. The Pradhan Mantri Fasal Bima Yojana, for which ₹ 9,000 crore have been allotted in the 2017-18 Union Budget is an important positive step towards risk mitigation for farmers but it needs to be subjected to four important reforms. First, at present, the insurance scheme limits the farmers' contribution towards premium to 1.5 percent to 2 percent of the sum insured for non-commercial crops and 5 percent of the sum insured for commercial crops irrespective of the sum insured. The government pays the remainder of the premium as subsidy. This model results in larger absolute subsidy amounts for larger farmers who are less vulnerable. The scheme should instead be modified to have a capped subsidy amount per farm household and any farmer desiring to insure larger sums should pay full premium for the difference. Second, insurance scheme should provide coverage for three to five years so that coverage extends to both good and bad years. Otherwise, insurance companies will have an incentive to go slow in selling policies during years that droughts are predicted. Third, the subsidy on the premium should take the form of direct benefit transfer to ensure that farmers can shop for the best value for their money. Finally, there should be minimally two companies offering insurance in any given location. This will create competition and lead to greater efficiency and lower premiums for farmers". [3]

6.8 Pradhan Mantri Kisan Samman Nidhi (PM-KISAN)

To provide an assured income support to the small and marginal farmers, the Finance Minister, while presenting Interim Budget for 2019-20 in the Parliament, announced a historic programme, namely PM-KISAN. Under this programme, vulnerable landholding farmer families, having cultivable land up to 2 hectares, will be provided direct income support at the rate of ₹ 6,000 per year. This income support will be transferred directly into the bank accounts of beneficiary farmers, in three equal instalments of ₹ 2,000 each. This programme will be funded by Government of India. Around 12 crore small and marginal farmer families are expected to benefit from this. The programme was made effective from December 1, 2018 and the first instalment for the period up to March 31, 2019 was paid during 2018-19 itself. This programme will entail an annual expenditure of ₹ 75,000 crore.

PM-KISAN not only provides assured supplemental income to the most vulnerable farmer families, but also meets their emergent needs especially before the harvest season. PM-KISAN paves the way for the farmers to earn and live a respectable living.

After assuming office for the second time on May 30, 2019, Prime Minister Narendra Modi chaired the first meeting of the Union Cabinet on May 31, 2019, and decided to extend PM-KISAN to allow all eligible farmers to avail benefit under this scheme. Thus, an estimated 2 crore more farmers were added to the scheme, taking the total number of beneficiaries to 14.5 crore.

In March 2020, in the wake of COVID-19, Government

transferred ₹ 17,986 crore to farmers under the PM-Kisan scheme. Instalments due for the period of April 1 to July 31, 2020 were paid to 8.13 crore beneficiaries.

6.9 Pradhan Mantri Kisan Maandhan Yojana (PMKMY)

PM-KMY was launched in September 2019 to expand the social security net to small and marginal farmers. It ensures minimum fixed pension of ₹ 3,000 to eligible landholding small and marginal farmers, on attaining the age of 60 years.

Endnotes

1. Government of India, Ministry of Finance, Budget Papers (2018-19), *Speech of the Finance Minister*, paras 13 to 15.
2. Government of India, Ministry of Finance, *Budget Speech of the Finance Minister 2017-18*, para 24.
3. NITI Aayog, *India: Three Year Action Agenda (2017-18 to 2019-20)*, August 2017, p. 32.

7

Crude Oil Prices and India

The oil resources of the world are unevenly distributed over the earth's surface and the concentration of reserves is usually not geographically coincided with the concentration of consumption. Hence, global energy trade remains dominated by crude oil and oil products.

7.1 Segments and Stakeholders in Petroleum Industry

The petroleum industry, also known as the oil industry, includes the global processes of exploration, extraction, refining, transporting (often by oil tankers and pipelines), and marketing of petroleum products.

7.1.1 Segments: Petroleum industry operates in three segments:

1. **Upstream:** The upstream segment covers all activities related to exploration and production.
2. **Midstream:** The midstream segment deals with storage and transportation of natural gas and crude oil.
3. **Downstream:** The downstream segment deals with fabrication and refining of petroleum products, storage, transportation and marketing of commodities like natural gas and crude oil.

7.1.2 Stakeholders: It is important to know the participants of the oil and natural gas industry to understand how petrol prices in India are determined. They include as under:

1. **Oil Exploration and Production Companies**: These companies are liable for producing oil in its crude form. The major participants of this segment include Crain India, Reliance Industries, Oil and Natural Gas Corporation (ONGC), Oil India. Only 15 percent of the country's crude

oil requirement is met through these companies and the rest through importing.

2. **Oil Marketing Companies:** Oil marketing companies, also called refineries, manage everything from the stage of crude oil till the delivery of saleable fuel to dealers. This segment consists of both public and private sector companies. Public sector companies include Indian Oil Corporation Limited (IOCL), Bharat Petroleum Corporation Limited (BPCL), Hindustan Petroleum Corporation Limited (HPCL), Numaligarh Refinery Limited (NRL), Mangalore Refinery and Petrochemicals Limited (MRPL) and Bharat Oman Refineries Ltd (BORL). Private sector companies include Reliance, Essar and shell. Excise duty is paid by OMCs before selling petrol to dealers.
3. **Dealers:** Owners of petrol pumps are called dealers who can be individuals or business entities. They sell petrol to end-users after adding their margins and local taxes.

Retail infrastructure includes terminals/depots, retail outlets, LPG bottling plants and LPG distributorships.

7.2 Crude Oil and Petroleum Products

7.2.1 Crude Oil: It is a naturally occurring fossil fuel. It is formed from ancient organic matter—such as plankton and algae—that has been buried underground and exposed to extreme heat and pressure. Crude is one of the world's most in-demand commodities, because it can be separated or refined into various consumer, industrial and energy products. These include gasoline (petrol), diesel, lubricants, wax, and other petrochemicals, many of which are used to manufacture plastics. The composition (or qualities) of crude oil varies by source, but there are two main high-quality types that are used to benchmark global prices. These standards are the United States' West Texas Intermediate (WTI) and United Kingdom's Brent crude.

7.2.2 Petroleum Products: Petroleum products are materials derived from crude oil (petroleum) as it is processed in oil refineries. Unlike petrochemicals, which are a collection of well-defined usually pure chemical compounds, petroleum products are complex mixtures. Crude oil is converted to petroleum products which include several classes of fuels.

According to the composition of the crude oil and depending on the demands of the market, refineries can produce different shares of petroleum products. The largest share of oil products is used as *energy carriers.* Fuels include petrol (also known as motor spirit or gasoline), diesel, jet fuel, kerosene, heating oil, and heavier fuel oils. Heavier (less volatile) fractions can also be used to produce asphalt, tar, paraffin wax, lubricating and other heavy oils.

Kerosene (also called paraffin), is a combustible liquid and utilised as a fuel for power, heat, light. It is usually a multi-purpose fuel and can be used effectively, carefully in order to get incredible results. Kerosene is famous among people for cost-effectiveness.

7.3 Natural Gas and Liquefied Petroleum Gas (LPG)

7.3.1 Natural Gas: Gas that is found under the ground or the sea and that is used as fuel is called natural gas. India imports half of its natural gas requirements.

1. **Compressed Natural Gas (CNG):** CNG, a fuel, can be utilised in lieu of propane, gasoline, diesel fuel. CNG ignition produces lesser detrimental gases than other fuels. In the event of a spill, it is harmless compared to other fuels. It can be discovered above oil repositories.
2. **Piped Natural Gas (PNG):** PNG is used for domestic, commercial and industrial consumption. PNG has several distinctions to its credit of being a pollution free, economical and safer fuel. PNG is supplied through pipe 24x7. PNG offers the convenience of ensuring continuous and adequate supply of PNG at all times, without any problems of storing gas in cylinders.

7.3.2 Liquefied Petroleum Gas (LPG): LPG is a composition of commercial propane and commercial butane. It is a fuel which is a mixture of gases kept in a liquid form by the pressure in a container. It can be extremely dangerous. The way it is utilised, shifted, and bottled should be paid extreme caution.

7.4 Crude Oil: Indigenous Production and Imports

The petroleum sector dominates India's current energy use. This is one of the most vulnerable sectors in the Indian energy scenario. As an oil deficit country, India is dependent upon imports of the crude oil from West Asian counties. India imports oil from 28 countries, though five countries—Nigeria, Saudi Arabia, UAE, Kuwait and Iran—account for more than 75 percent of the total oil imports. The Persian Gulf region alone supplies more than 67 percent of India's needs.

From Table 7.1 it is clear that India's dependence on imported crude oil is not only high but also increasing year by year.

Table 7.1: Indigenous Production and Import of Crude Oil in Recent Years

(million tonnes)

Year	Production	Imports	Total	Col. 3 as percent of Col. 4
1	2	3	4	5
2012-13	38	185	223	82.9
2013-14	38	189	227	83.2
2014-15	37	189	226	83.6
2015-16	37	203	240	84.6
2016-17	36	214	251	85.2
2017-18	36	220	256	86.9
2018-19	34	227	261	87.0

Source: Reserve Bank of India, *Handbook of Statistics on Indian Economy, 2018-19*, Table 34 (excerpted).

India is the third biggest importers of crude oil after China and Japan. The indigenous crude oil production will have to be augmented by acceleration of exploration efforts in deep off-shore, unexplored/less explored off-shore as well as on-shore areas, improving reservoir management and enhanced oil recovery. Government must continue to encourage national and international oil companies to come and explore for oil and gas in the country. New technology to extract more oil from known or depleted reserves should also be encouraged.

The average recovery factor in India is low by international standards. An improvement in the recovery factor would give additional amount of oil without corresponding accretion of reserves. Simultaneously, exploration and development projects need to be taken up in other countries.

Pressing concerns about energy security have pushed states across the world into resource search frenzy, and India is no exception. India—being the world's sixth largest energy consumer in the wake of robust economic development, industrialization, rising population and rapidly growing number of vehicles on the road—needs a comprehensive energy security regime. Around 30 percent of India's energy requirements are met through oil. India's dependence on oil supplies from the Gulf countries makes it vulnerable to oil shocks. In this context, India is continuously reviewing and amending its energy policies and also searching for alternative supplies overseas. The growing pace of the Indian economy has not only led to a rise in energy consumption but a shift in its energy mix too.

Improved energy efficiency and technological changes, including the rise of renewable energy sources may slow down the demand for crude oil in the long-run.

India is expected to overtake Japan and Russia and become the third largest consumer of energy by the year 2030. The increasing political instability in the Middle East region has adversely impacted the energy security and it has gained centrality in the current international debates. In order for India to maintain the current trends in its economic growth, it must ensure energy security. India's current energy component is coal dominant and oil accounts for almost a third. The bulk of oil is imported, especially from Middle Eastern countries, which is primarily consumed in the transport sector.

7.5 What Determines Global Crude Oil Prices?

With each passing year, oil seems to play an even greater role in the global economy. Like all commodities, the price of crude oil in the international market is determined by demand and supply factors. If the worldwide demand for crude oil is high, and supply low, oil prices will be high. Demand and supply forces, in turn, are influenced by a host of factors.

7.5.1 Demand Factors: These can be as under:

1. Demand for oil generally depends on overall global economic growth as the commodity has wide-ranging applications. Demand often increases during boom periods and falls when the world economy is performing poorly.
2. Oil is traditionally priced in US dollars so demand can also be influenced by the relative strength or weakness of this particular currency, even becoming more attractive as an investment when the dollar is weak.
3. Demand for alternative energy sources, which compete with oil in certain markets, can also have an effect.
4. Demand also depends on weather conditions in Europe (severe cold means more heating and hence more demand for oil).
5. Crude inventory levels in US and other major oil-consuming countries also affect demand for crude oil.

7.5.2 Supply Factors: Global reserves of oil are limited and will eventually run out. Current supply of oil is largely dependent on how much countries are willing or able to drill. There are host of factors which determine the global supply of crude oil.

A. Political Factors: Crude oil prices are affected by wars, terrorist attacks, and civil strife (as in Libya). American sanctions on Iran, hyper inflation in Venezuela, fear of escalation in trade war, especially between US and China are other examples of political factors.

Early 2018, US had withdrawn from the 2015 Iranian

nuclear deal and re-imposed a series of tough sanctions on Iran which came into full force on November 4, 2018 and the US expected all countries, including India, to bring down their imports of Iranian oil to zero by then. The US had made it clear that any country that continues to do business with Iran would be blocked from accessing American banking and financial system.

US sanctions on Iran are not endorsed by the United Nations. It has been a traditional policy of India to endorse only UN Security Council authorized sanctions. Though India, one of the biggest importers of Iranian oil, has already reduced its imports, it has indicated that it is unlikely to go down to zero imports given its massive energy needs.

B. Natural Calamities and Seasonal and Weather Conditions: Seasonal conditions in oil producing countries have a direct impact on extracting raw oil. Oil producing companies cannot have the same productivity throughout all seasons. A drop in productivity gives a boost to the buying cost of raw oil at global markets.

Supply is disrupted due to weather conditions also. Oil platforms in the sea are evacuated whenever there is anticipation/warning of cyclone, hurricane, tsunami etc. Supply remains suspended till weather is normalized.

Crude oil once purchased by oil companies is transported to refineries. When bad weather reports interrupt transportation activities, crude oil supply is adversely affected.

C. Role of Organization for Petroleum Exporting Countries (OPEC): Probably the single biggest influencer of crude oil prices is OPEC, made up of 13 countries (Algeria, Angola, Ecuador, Indonesia, Iran, Iraq, Kuwait, Libya, Nigeria, Qatar, Saudi Arabia, the United Arab Emirates and Venezuela). Collectively, OPEC controls 40 percent of the world's supply of oil. This body sets production quotas for its members, with the aim of reducing competition and keeping prices at profitable levels.

OPEC was founded in the 1960 to fix oil and gas prices.

By restricting production, OPEC can force prices to rise, and thereby enjoy greater profits than if its member countries sell independently in the world market. Throughout the 1970s and much of the 1980s, OPEC followed this sound, if somewhat unethical, strategy.

Of late, OPEC is becoming limited in its ability to influence global crude oil prices. OPEC member countries often exceed their quotas, selling a few million extra barrels knowing that enforcers cannot really stop them from doing so. Similarly, non-members Canada, China, Russia and USA are increasing their own output.

Technological advancements and deregulations in recent years have seen increased USA shale oil production, leading to a shift in the balance of global supply from OPEC to the US.

D. Government Policies: Government policies and regulations in different countries regarding oil exploration, exports and imports may change from time-to-time and hence influence the supply of crude oil.

7.5.3 Other Factors: These can include the following:

A. Oil Futures Market: In fact, the price of oil is set in the oil futures market. An oil futures contract is a binding agreement that gives one the right to purchase oil by the barrel at a pre-defined price on a pre-defined date in the future. Under a futures contract, both the buyer and the seller are obligated to fulfil their side of the transaction on the specified date.

The following are two types of futures traders:

1. **Hedgers:** An example of a hedger would be an airline buying oil futures to guard against potential price rise.
2. **Speculators:** An example of a speculator would be someone who is just guessing the price direction and has no intention of actually buying the product. Majority of futures trading is done by speculators because very rarely their transactions actually result in the purchaser of a futures contract taking possession of the commodity being traded.

B. Sentiments: The other key factor in determining oil prices is sentiment. The mere belief that oil demand will increase dramatically at some point in the future can result in increase in oil prices in the present as speculators and hedgers alike snap up oil futures contracts. Of course, the opposite is also true. The mere belief that oil demand will decrease at some point in the future can result in a dramatic decrease in prices in the present as oil futures contracts are sold. Thus, crude oil prices hinge on market psychology at times.

Basic demand and supply theory states that more of a product is produced, the more cheaply it should sell, other things being equal. However, there are other factors also which determine the price of crude oil in the global market.

7.6 COVID-19, Worldwide Lockdowns and Fall in Crude Oil Prices

Crude oil ruled at US$ 147 per barrel (highest in history) in August 2009.

At the beginning of 2020, global oil market was experiencing high oil output as a result of production increases in US, Canada, and some other non-OPEC+ countries. With COVID-19 outbreak in China, and the lockdown of Wuhan, a major industrial hub, oil prices tumbled down from US$ 68 per barrel in early January 2020 to US$ 53 per barrel in early February 2020.

In February 2020, Saudi Arabia increased crude oil output after Russia refused to deepen production cuts in line with an earlier OPEC supply pact.

In mid-March 2020, Saudi Arabia announced it would pump a record 12.3 million barrel per day (mbpd), unleashing the so-called price war with Russia. The explosion of supply came as governments worldwide announced lockouts, crushing fuel demand.

As the outbreak grew into a pandemic, countries around the world were affected, causing panic and unplanned lockouts. Industries were shut down and transport and travel activities came to a screeching halt. This led to fall in oil prices and price war (in the form of discounts) among major oil exporters.

Since the falling oil prices were hurting the US shale oil industry, President Trump intervened and pressed Saudi Arabia to end its oil price war with Russia, and arranged, on April 12, 2020, what came to be called OPEC+ deal. Under this deal, oil exporting countries agreed to cut down their total oil production by 9.7 million barrel per day (mbpd) during the months of May and June 2020. The deal (largest production cut ever negotiated) came into effect on May 1, 2020. It was supposed to help stabilize prices. In view of the worldwide lockdowns which were extended by most countries, the deal-induced decrease in oil production proved insufficient to halt and possibly reverse the falling oil prices. Oil prices started hovering around US$ 20 per barrel, causing immense harm to oil-dependent countries of Persian Gulf.

7.6.1 Reversal of Oil Price Policy of US: America has a strong desire to protect its oil industry. Not long ago US always criticised supply cuts by OPEC and other oil exporting countries because such actions raised energy costs for Americans. It always wanted low oil prices which it believed were akin to tax cuts.

Now, President Trump is asking OPEC, led by Saudi Arabia, to slash output so that oil prices are higher enough to sustain commercial viability of US shale oil companies.

After the discovery of shale oil it has changed its position. Shale oil industry in US is commercial viable at a particular international price of crude oil (around US$ 40 per barrel). Hence, US wants lower crude oil prices but not below US$ 40 to protect its shale oil industry.

US can pressurize Saudi Arabia because the latter depends on the former for its security and stability. US is reportedly stationing 3,000 troops in Saudi Arabia. It has installed Patriot missiles and anti-missile defence systems there. US navy's Fifth Fleet protects oil exports from the kingdom. Saudi Arabia relies on US for weapons and protection against regional rivals such as Iran.

COVID-related crash in international prices of crude oil and petroleum products has proved a windfall for petroleum importing countries, mainly China, Japan and India.

7.7 Impact of Global Crude Oil Prices on India

US dollar is the base currency to buy raw oil. With oil's stature as a high-demand global commodity comes the possibility that major fluctuations in price can have a significant economic impact.

7.7.1 Rising Prices: Higher crude oil prices adversely impact India in at least three ways.

1. Domestic demand is reduced and so also the growth rate of the economy.
2. Rate of inflation increases.
3. Current account deficit (CAD) in the balance of payments is widened.

According to *Economic Survey, 2017-18*, "It is estimated that a US$ 10 per barrel increase in the price of oil reduces growth by 0.2-0.3 percentage points, increases WPI inflation by about 1.7 percentage points and worsens the CAD by about US$ 9-10 billion dollars". [1]

Increase in petrol and diesel prices may pinch consumers hard but they also promote more and more vehicle owners to switch to clean-burning CNG

7.7.2 Falling Prices: Fall in global crude oil prices have advantages as well as disadvantages for the Indian economy.

A. Advantages: With 80 percent dependence on imports to meet domestic oil requirements, any reduction in international crude oil prices proves a windfall for India. Import bill comes down, making current account deficit in the balance of payments more manageable.

Cheaper imported crude oil means cheaper final products (mainly petrol and diesel). Keeping excise duty on final products unchanged, Government can pass on the benefit to consumers by lowering retail prices of petrol and diesel. It helps to lower the rate of inflation. Lower prices of petroleum products also mean lower subsidies on kerosene and cooking gas which, in turn, help to reduce budgetary deficit (or more appropriately revenue deficit).

If retail prices of petrol and diesel stay at current level (i.e. benefit is not passed on), scope for higher excise duties is widened. Centre can raise excise duty on petrol/diesel to soak up the benefit of a sharp fall in crude oil prices without putting extra burden on consumers. It can simply ask the state-run oil companies to adjust the enhanced excise duty against their hefty profit margins.

Government has followed a mixed approach of benefiting the consumers and generating more revenues for the exchequer.

B. Disadvantages: Falling crude prices adversely hit government revenues in oil-exporting countries, particularly in the Middle-East. This may reduce demand for India's exports. If exports from India are adversely hit, it could pose a set back for *Make in India* plans of the Government.

If international crude oil prices fall, many expatriates (mainly from India, Pakistan and Bangladesh) may lose their jobs in the Middle-East, resulting into reduced level of remittances which are a major source of foreign exchange earnings. India is the biggest recipient of remittances in the world from non-resident Indians. However, the level of remittances depends upon political and economic conditions in the Middle East and other countries where Indian Diaspora is settled.

For example, more than a third of Oman's 4.6 million residents are expatriates, mainly from India, Pakistan and Bangladesh. About 8 lakh Indians work in Omen On April 29, 2020, Finance Ministry of Oman instructed government-owned companies to replace foreign workers with locals as part of efforts to develop national workforce. This so-called Omanisation Policy is likely to be extended to private companies as well.

The return of several thousand of migrants from the Gulf countries will have a huge adverse impact on the Indian economy.

On April 22, 2020, World Bank predicted sharpest decline of remittances in recent history. Global remittances are estimated to decline by about 20 percent in 2020 due to the economic crisis induced by COVID-19 pandemic. The projected fall will be largely a fall in wages and employment of migrant workers, who tend to be more vulnerable to loss of employment and wages during an economic crisis in a host country. India's foreign remittances are likely to go down by 23 percent.

Low oil prices can make many new projects of oil producers in India, such as ONGC and Oil India Limited unviable. Low oil prices can lead to volatility in global markets with a contagion effect on India's markets.

On balance, however, benefits of lower crude oil prices to India seem to outweigh the negatives.

7.8 Future Scenario

Oil demand recovery is expected to be slow and dependent on the dynamics of COVID-19 pandemic. If there is no second wave outbreak, the recovery will be faster otherwise not.

Even if the demand for oil recovers, it may not push up prices, because countries will be using extra barrels of oil accumulated in their reserves during distress sale prices. How sincerely oil producers, who are part of OPEC+ deal, adhere to the requirements of the deal is another moot question.

Although the world economy may start to recover as more countries allow businesses to reopen, prospects for crude oil prices remain gloomy. Supply cuts are not deep enough to counter plummeting demand. Crude oil prices are likely to remain low at least for one year due mainly to two reasons: (a) exhausted global storage capacity and (b) frail demand, i.e. demand may be slow to recover even after countries ease restrictions to combat the coronavirus pandemic.

In short, low crude oil prices are here to stay for long.

Endnote

1. Government of India, *Economic Survey, 2017-18*, Volume I, p. 18.

8

Ease of Doing Business in India: Recent Improved Rankings

In the development strategy adopted after Independence in 1947, India paid little attention to improve business environment. As a consequence, entrepreneurs struggled to do business in the face of restrictive policies and regulations that were designed to choke rather than enable business. Myriad rules and regulations inhibited business growth and held back India from achieving its potential. Economic reforms initiated in 1991 marked a clear change in direction as successive governments started paying attention to difficulties faced by businesses. Although the situation has improved considerably in recent years yet India remains a tough place to do business as per benchmarks of developed countries.

8.1 Why is it Difficult to Do Business in India?

As a large, labour-abundant economy, one would expect India to have a comparative advantage in large-scale, labour-intensive manufacturing. Yet, India has not done well in this sector. Instead, successful sectors in India have been either capital- or skilled labour-intensive and most prominently include auto, auto parts, two wheelers, automobiles, engineering goods, petroleum refining, pharmaceuticals and software. Labour-intensive products such as apparel, footwear, food processing, furniture and various other light manufactures have not flourished in India. Analysts have often pointed to regulatory burden, rigid labour laws and deficient infrastructure as possible reasons for this puzzle.

In India's federal set up, business regulations are enacted and implemented by all three tiers of governance—central, state and municipalities. The huge labyrinth of business regulations across the country has raised the compliance burden to such levels of deterrence that existing businesses are reluctant to expand while starts-ups are few and far between. At the municipality level, construction permits take long time to materialize. Challenges faced in getting utility connections, such as electricity and water at the State Government level, are formidable. Environmental clearances are equally testing at both the State and the Central level and so are the statutes and inspections under labour legislations. In view of regulatory hurdles and red tape, India was traditionally seen as a country not friendly for domestic and foreign investors.

Although licensing controls and discretionary approvals have been greatly reduced yet there are many remnants of the control regime that need drastic overhaul. Quantitative controls, where they exist, should give way to fiscal measures and increased reliance on competitive markets subject to appropriate, transparent and effective regulations. The burden of multiple inspections by government agencies must be removed and tax regimes rationalized.

8.2 World Bank's Doing Business Report

Doing Business Report is a flagship annual publication of the World Bank. It looks at domestic small and medium-sized companies and measures the regulations applying to them through their life cycle. Doing business captures several important dimensions of the regulatory environment as it applies to local firms. The purpose of *Doing Business Report* is to provide objective data for use by governments in designing sound business regulatory policies and to encourage research on the important dimensions of the regulatory environment for firms.

The first *Doing Business Report*, published in 2003, covered 5 indicators and 133 economies. The 2020 Report provided quantitative indicators covering 12 areas of business environment in 190 economies. Only 10 indicators out of 12 were used in the 2020 Report.

The 12 indicators with brief explanations are as under:

1. **Starting a Business:** Procedures, time, cost and paid-in minimum capital to start a limited liability company.
2. **Employing Workers:** The employing workers indicator set measures regulation in the areas of hiring, working hours, and redundancy.
3. **Dealing with Construction Permits:** Procedures, time and cost to complete all formalities to build a warehouse and the quality control and safety mechanisms in the construction permitting system.
4. **Getting Electricity:** Procedures, time and cost to get connected to the electrical grid, the reliability of the electricity supply and the transparency of tariffs.
5. **Registering Property:** Procedures, time and cost to transfer a property and the quality of the land administration system.
6. **Getting Credit**: Movable collateral laws and credit information systems.
7. **Protecting Minority Investors:** Minority shareholders' rights in related-party transactions and in corporate governance.
8. **Paying Taxes**: Payments, time and total tax rate for a firm to comply with all tax regulations as well as post-filing processes.
9. **Trading Across Borders:** Time and cost to export the product of comparative advantage and import auto parts.
10. **Contracting with the Government:** The contracting with the government indicators capture the time and procedures involved in a standardized public procurement for road resurfacing.
11. **Enforcing Contracts:** Time and cost to resolve a commercial dispute and the quality of judicial processes.
12. **Resolving Insolvency**: Time, cost, outcome and recovery rate for a commercial insolvency and the strength of the legal framework for insolvency.

The World Bank—which popularised the exercise of

ranking countries according to the ease of doing business—gathers and analyses comprehensive quantitative data to compare business regulation environments across economies and over time, *Doing Business Report*: (a) encourages economies to compete towards more efficient regulations, (b) offers measurable benchmarks for reforms and (c) serves as a resource for academics, journalists, private sector researchers and others interested in the business climate of each economy.

In addition, *Doing Business Report* offers detailed sub-national reports, which exhaustively cover business regulations and reforms in different cities and regions within a country. These reports: (a) provide data on the ease of doing business, (b) rank each location and (c) recommend reforms to improve performance in each of the indicator areas. Selected cities can compare their business regulations with other cities in the economy or region and with the 190 economies ranked by the World Bank.

Doing Business Report relies on four main sources of information: the relevant laws and regulations, Doing Business respondents, the governments of the economies covered and World Bank Group regional staff. Responses are sought from experts, chartered accountants, lawyers and other professionals. [1]

Doing Business data are widely used by governments, researchers, international organizations and think tanks to guide policies, conduct research and develop new indexes.

8.3 Highlights of Doing Business Report, 2020

Doing Business, 2020, was the 17th in a series of annual studies investigating the regulations that enhance business activity and those that constrain it. Doing Business presented quantitative indicators on business regulations and the protection of property rights that can be compared across 190 economies—from Afghanistan to Zimbabwe—and over time.

Regulations affecting 10 areas of the life of a business were covered: starting a business, dealing with construction permits, getting electricity, registering property, getting credit, protecting minority investors, paying taxes, trading across borders, enforcing contracts, and resolving insolvency.

1. Data in Doing Business 2020 were as of May 1, 2019.
2. The indicators were used to analyze economic outcomes and identify what reforms of business regulation had worked, where and why.
3. The study showed that developing economies were catching up with developed economies in ease of doing business.
4. Worldwide, 115 economies made it easier to do business.
5. The economies with the most notable improvement in doing business were Saudi Arabia, Jordan, Togo, Bahrain, Tajikistan, Pakistan, Kuwait, China, India, and Nigeria.
6. Only two African economies rank in the top 50 on the ease of doing business;
7. Research demonstrated a causal relationship between economic freedom and gross domestic product (GDP) growth.

Table 8.1 depicts ease of doing business rankings of top ten countries of the world plus those of China, India and Pakistan.

China improved its ranking from 90 in 2015 to 31 in 2020, a leap of 59 spots. India improved its ranking from 142 in 2015 to 63 in 2020, a jump of 79 spots. Pakistan is way behind both China and India in terms of ease of doing business (Table 8.2).

8.4 Doing Business Ranking of India in Recent Years

As per the World Bank's Doing Business Report, 2015, India ranked 142 among 189 countries in terms of ease of doing business. India ranked even below Pakistan which occupied 128th rank and much below China which occupied 90th rank. With the exception of two parameters (*getting credit* and *protecting minority investors*), India did not feature in the top 100 in the remaining parameters. In *dealing with construction permits* and *enforcing contracts* parameters, India ranked in the bottom 10 economies as per the ranking.

Table 8.1: Ease of Doing Business Rankings, 2020
Top Ten Countries of the World plus China, India and Pakistan

Country	Ease of doing business rank*	Score (out of 100)**
New Zealand	1 (1)	86.8 (86.59)
Singapore	2 (2)	86.2 (85.24)
Hong Kong	3 (4)	85.3 (84.22)
Denmark	4 (3)	85.3 (84.64)
South Korea	5 (5)	84.0 (84.14)
USA	6 (8)	84.0 (82.75)
Georgia	7 (6)	83.7 (83.28)
UK	8 (9)	83.5 (82.65)
Norway	9 (7)	82.6 (82.95)
Sweden	10 (***)	82.0 (***)
China	**31 (46)**	**77.9 (73.64)**
India	**63 (77)**	**71.0 (67.23)**
Pakistan	**108 (136)**	**61.0 (55.31)**

*Figures in parentheses indicate ranking in 2019.
**Figures in parentheses indicate score in 2019.
***Not in top ten in 2019.
Note: A high *ease of doing business* ranking means the regulatory environment is more conducive to the starting and operation of a local firm.
Source: World Bank, *Doing Business*, 2019 and 2020.

Table 8.2: Ease of Doing Business Ranks of China, India and Pakistan in Recent Years

Country	**2015**	**2017**	**2018**	**2019**	**2020**
China	90	78	78	46	31
India	142	130	100	77	63
Pakistan	128	142	147	136	108

Source: World Bank, *Doing Business Report* (various years).

India's overall ranking and the individual rankings in various parameters clearly showed that India was in urgent need of reforms to unlock the huge economic potential of the country. However, the reforms needed to be initiated at various levels across Centre, State and local governments. Bold and necessary reforms in various areas were needed to herald an era of high value investments, infrastructure growth, job creation, skill development and economic prosperity. As a result of reforms at various levels, India has come up well to occupy 63rd rank in the 2020 Report.

India was ranked at 130 in the 2017 Report.

2018 report was the 15th in a series of annual reports investigating the regulations that enhance business activity and those which constrain it. India was ranked at 100th position. India made a very significant jump, improving its rank from 130th in 2017 to 100th in 2018. This improvement of 30 ranks to break into the top 100 reflected Government's reform measures on a wide range of indicators.

India saw an improvement in the following six out of ten indicators:

1. Dealing with construction permits.
2. Getting credit.
3. Protecting minority investors.
4. Paying taxes.
5. Enforcing contracts.
6. Resolving insolvency.

India improved in the above areas on the back of administrative reforms in taxation and passage of the Insolvency and Bankruptcy Code (IBC), 2016. These improvements in rankings were a result of various reform measures undertaken by the Government including structural and deep-seated reforms. It is noteworthy that these were exactly the areas where India had traditionally done very poorly.

This had prompted the Government to initiate a slew of business-friendly institutional reforms including Make-in-India, simplification of tax procedures, bankruptcy laws and so on. All of these led to the big jump in India's ranking.

In the 2019 report, India was placed at 77 in World Bank's Doing Business Report 2019, making it the highest-ranked South Asian country.

In the 2020 report, India moved from 77th to 63rd position. This jump of 14 ranks was primarily driven by significant improvements in 7 out of 10 factors on which ease of doing business was measured. The 2020 Doing Business Report observed as under:

1. **Starting a Business:** India made starting a business easier by abolishing filing fees for the SPICe company incorporation form, electronic memorandum of association, and articles of association. This reform applies to both Delhi and Mumbai.
2. **Dealing with Construction Permits:** India (Delhi) streamlined the process, reduced the time and cost of obtaining construction permits, and improved building quality control by strengthening professional certification requirements. India (Mumbai) streamlined the process of obtaining a building permit and made it faster and less expensive to get a construction permit.
3. **Trading Across Borders**: India made trading across borders easier by enabling post-clearance audits, integrating trade stakeholders in a single electronic platform, upgrading port infrastructures, and enhancing the electronic submission of documents. This reform applies to both Delhi and Mumbai.
4. **Resolving Insolvency**: India made resolving insolvency easier by promoting reorganization proceedings in practice. India also made resolving insolvency more difficult by not allowing dissenting creditors to receive as much under reorganization as they would receive in liquidation. This reform applies to both Delhi and Mumbai.

Thus, the country has performed remarkably well by jumping 79 places since 2015. The improved ranking has enhanced India's global image as a promising investment destination.

8.5 High, Moderate and Low Rank Indicators of India

Prime Minister Narendra Modi vowed to break into the top

50 by 2020 when he took over in 2014. Though the ranking in 2020 came very close to the target but it failed to achieve it. To improve its position, India should look at areas where it needs to change. Since there are 10 parameters in the rankings, and all parameters have equal weightage, it is easy to pick the ones where India does not fair well.

8.5.1 India's High Rank Indicators: These are as under:

1. Dealing with construction permits.
2. Getting electricity.
3. Getting credit.
4. Protecting minority investors.

8.5.2 India's Moderate Rank Indicators: These are the following:

1. Trading across borders.
2. Resolving insolvency.

8.5.3 India's Low Rank Indicators: These are as under:

1. Starting a business.
2. Registering property.
3. Paying taxes.
4. Enforcing contracts.

India continues to lag on the indicator of enforcing contracts. The importance of an effective, efficient and expeditious contract enforcement regime to economic growth and development cannot be overstated. A clear and certain legislative and executive regime backed by an efficient judiciary that fairly and punctually protects property rights, preserves sanctity of contracts, and enforces the rights and liabilities of parties is a prerequisite for business and commerce.

In connection with contract enforcement, the *Economic Survey, 2017-18* observed, "The Government has taken a number of actions to expedite and improve the contract enforcement regime. For example, the Government: scrapped over 1,000 redundant legislations; rationalized tribunals; amended The Arbitration and Conciliation Act, 2015; passed The Commercial Courts, Commercial Division and

Commercial Appellate Division of High Courts Act, 2015; reduced intra-government litigation; and expanded the Lok Adalat Programme to reduce the burden on the judiciary. The government has also advanced a prospective legislative regime to ensure legal consistency, reducing chaos due to unpredictable changes in regulations. The judiciary has simultaneously expanded the seminal National Judicial Data Grid (NJDG) and is close to ensuring that every High Court of the country is digitized". [2]

8.6 Reforms Introduced in India as per Doing Business Reports of World Bank: 2008 to 2020

See appendix to this book.

8.7 Recent Measures to Improve Business Environment in India

The present Central Government led by Prime Minister Narendra Modi has made ease of doing business—especially for small and medium enterprises—a clear area of focus. Likewise, State Governments are also taking business facilitation measures to attract investment and enterprise to their respective States. This competitive federalism—which taps into the competitive instincts of the States—offers a powerful framework within which India can reform its business environment. Therefore, reforms at the state level are as crucial as reforms by the Central Government. This is especially true in the context of numerous clearances/filings which small and medium enterprises must obtain/comply with to start and run businesses.

State Governments have initiated significant procedural and policy reforms to promote foreign investment and encourage domestic private participation in the development of their respective States. While the incentive package varies from State to State depending upon their investment priorities, some common features are discernible. These include development of industrial estates, removing artificial barriers within States, decentralisation of decision-making, time-bound clearance of projects, investment subsidy, and power tariff concessions.

If states are to effectively compete and trigger a virtuous cycle of economic activity, they need to know whether enterprises are successfully taking advantage of the changes they are making to improve the environment. They also need to better understand the relationship of the business environment to growth and job creation.

Recent measures to promote and facilitate business initiatives have included the following:

1. Companies (Amendment) Act, 2015 has been passed to remove requirements of minimum paid-up capital and common seal for companies.
2. An investor facilitation cell has been created under Invest India to guide, assist and handhold investors during the entire life-cycle of the business.
3. The process of applying for environment and forest clearances has been made online through the Ministry of Environment, Forests and Climate Change portals.
4. Registration with the Employees Provident Fund Organization (EPFO) and Employees State Insurance Corporation (ESIC) has been automated and ESIC registration number is being provided on a real-time basis.
5. A unified portal for registration of units for labour identification number (LIN), reporting of inspection, submission of returns and grievance redressal has been launched by the Ministry of Labour and Employment.
6. The Insolvency and Bankruptcy Code (IBC), 2016 was passed in May 2016. Since then, the entire mechanism for the Corporate Insolvency Resolution Process (CIRP) has been put in place. A number of rules and regulations have been notified to create the institutions and professionals necessary for the process to work. A large number of cases have entered the insolvency process.
7. India introduced a comprehensive Goods and Services Tax

(GST) on July 1, 2017. Prior to the introduction of GST, the indirect tax system of India suffered from various disabilities. There was a burden of *tax-on-tax* in the pre-GST system of Central excise duty and the sales tax (later VAT) system of the States. GST is a tax on goods and services with comprehensive and continuous chain of set-off benefits up to the retailer level. It is essentially a tax only on value addition at each stage, and a supplier at each stage is permitted to set-off, through a tax credit mechanism, the GST paid on the purchase of goods and services.

To sum up, in recent years, Central and State Governments have embarked upon a transformational journey of improving India's business climate. A multitude of reforms have been unveiled to improve business environment. Resultantly, India is being viewed by global investors as the economic power house of the future.

Regulatory reforms are but a stepping stone towards greater investment. The private sector in India faces many challenges, and the regulatory burden is just one of them. Infrastructure and finance related challenges can be as severe as regulatory burdens in discouraging investment. More complex reforms may need to be undertaken to bring about a paradigm shift in investment.

To ensure that the private sector is aware of the reforms that have happened, Central and State Governments should undertake communications campaigns to inform businesses about their reforms. Proactive communication can be instrumental not only in generating awareness, but also in increasing usage and uptake of the reformed services. Awareness and increased usage will also allow businesses to test the effectiveness of the measures and incentivize them to report on problems.

Endnotes

1. Similarly, in India, the Department of Industrial Policy and Promotion (DIPP), Ministry of Commerce and Industry,

Government of India bases its ranking of states on the responses of State Governments on whether or not they have implemented the DIPP-recommended best practices in different areas. The approach taken by the World Bank largely tells the story from the viewpoint of experts who closely follow the developments in business environment and that by DIPP from the viewpoint of the implementing agencies.

2. Government of India, *Economic Survey, 2017-18*, Volume I, p. 132.

9

Infrastructure and Logistics Development

9.1 Infrastructure Services

Provision of quality infrastructure services at reasonable cost is a necessary condition for achieving sustained economic growth. In fact, one of the major challenges being faced by the Indian economy is to enhance infrastructure investment and to improve the delivery system and quality of services. Investment in infrastructure involves high risk, low return, lumpiness of huge investment, high incremental capital/output ratio, long payback periods and superior technology. These prerequisites pose a constraint on the Government's efficient delivery of quality infrastructure services. Government is moving away from its traditional role as a *provider* of services to one of *facilitator* and *regulator* by ensuring that infrastructure services are actually delivered in a desirable manner.

Infrastructure is generally defined as the physical framework of facilities through which goods and services are provided to the public. Its linkages to the economy are multiple and complex, because it affects production and consumption directly, creates positive and negative spill over effects (externalities), and involves large flows of expenditure.

In economic literature, infrastructure is popular by the name *overhead capital* which represents basic services without which primary, secondary and tertiary productive activities cannot function. The very success of social and economic transformation of an economy lies in providing inclusive and sustainable infrastructure amenities to the people and the pace of economic growth depends on how competently and judiciously an economy is able to address its infrastructure bottlenecks.

Infrastructure has, inter alia, the following distinct components: (a) energy, (b) transport, (c) telecommunications, (d) irrigation, (e) water supply and sanitation.

The availability of adequate infrastructure facilities is imperative for the overall economic development of a country. Infrastructure adequacy helps determine success in diversifying production, expanding trade, coping with population growth, reducing poverty and improving environmental conditions. Infrastructure contributes to economic development both by increasing productivity and by providing amenities which enhance the quality of life. The services provided lead to growth in production in several ways.

1. Infrastructure services are intermediate inputs to privatisation and any reduction in these input costs raises the profitability of production, thus permitting higher levels of output, income, and/or employment.
2. They raise the productivity of other factors, including labour and other capital. Infrastructure is thereby often described as an 'unpaid' factor of production, since its availability leads to higher returns obtainable from other capital and labour.

Prime Minister Narendra Modi announced on May 12, 2020, the Aatmanirbhar Bharat Abhiyan (Self-reliant India Movement) to cope with the situation created by Covid-19 pandemic. A mega package of ₹ 20 lakh crore (10 percent of GDP) was announced for the purpose.

The details of the 20 lakh crore package were announced by Finance Minister Nirmala Sitharaman in five tranches during the next five consecutive days. All the measures were aimed at spurring investment and buffering the economy against the COVID-19 shock.

On May 16, 2020 Government announced the fourth set of measures which included a major opening up of coal, defence production, civil aviation, power, space, social infrastructure and atomic energy for private participation. The measures announced were intended to signal India's readiness to proactively seek investment and instil confidence in business circles.

For details, see chapter 4 of this book.

9.2 Logistics Services and Support

Logistics refers to a series of services and activities, such as transportation, warehousing, and brokerage that help to move goods and establish supply chains across and within borders. Although these services and activities are carried out by private firms for the benefit of private firms, service delivery and the efficiency of supply chains depend on public sector provisions and interventions in a number of domains. Logistics uses publicly funded or regulated infrastructure. International trade is processed by border agencies. Services and logistics activities are regulated with fiscal, environmental, safety, land use, and competition objectives.

Logistics organizes the movement of goods through a network of activities and services operating at global, regional, and local scale. Logistics encompasses more than freight transportation. Traders delegate increasingly sophisticated tasks to networks of specialized service providers. Efficient logistics connects people and firms to markets and opportunities and helps achieve higher levels of productivity and welfare. Crucially, logistics is not only a private endeavour, but also a public policy concern. The performance and reliability of supply chains depend on an array of interventions, ranging from trade facilitation at the border to infrastructure and regulations and to urban planning and skills. Empirical evidence confirms that logistics and connectivity-related interventions have the highest potential to reduce the cost of trade and to boost integration in global value chains. Policy makers know that logistics matters and that they can improve the efficiency of the supply chains connecting their countries internally and externally.

Logistics is the backbone of a country's economy and development. With India's growing economy, it is imperative to invest in robust logistics infrastructure and efficient supply chains. The success of Government of India's 'Make in India' initiative rests heavily on an efficient logistics system. The objective of 'Make in India' is to strengthen India's manufacturing sector and build state of the art manufacturing infrastructure in the country. To support this vision, logistics and supply chain can be improved and made more efficient.

The status of logistics as a policy concern is now firmly established. Not only private sector executives, but also policy makers across all types of countries are aware of the contribution of efficient supply chains to the national economy.

Reliable logistics is indispensable to integrate global value chains—and reap the benefit of trade opportunities for growth and poverty reduction. The ability to connect to the global logistics web depends on a country's infrastructure, service markets, and trade processes. Government and the private sector in many developing countries should improve these areas—or face the large and growing costs of exclusion.

9.2.1 World Bank's Logistics Performance Index (LPI): Based on a worldwide survey of global freight forwarders and express carriers, LPI is a benchmarking tool developed by the World Bank that measures performance along the logistics supply chain within a country. Allowing for comparisons across 160 countries, the index can help countries to identify challenges and opportunities and improve their logistics performance. The World Bank conducts the survey every two years. The LPI is unique as a tool of decision making since it expresses the perception of operators on the ground; this is often as important as hard statistical data.

LPI is instrumental in the policy choices of governments, non-governmental organizations, and private enterprises worldwide, and the visibility of the freight forwarding and logistics sector as an intrinsic arm of global trade and commerce is crucial. There is no trade without logistics, and poor logistics often means poor trade. It needs to be emphasized that moving goods across borders is not the be-all and end-all of logistics performance, which requires the integration of many elements throughout the entire supply chain. The challenge is to ensure that the LPI and all the insight into markets it contains reaches decision-makers not only in the public sector but also in the private sector.

Now in its sixth edition (2007, 2010, 2012, 2014, 2016 and 2018), LPI embodies the experience of logistics professionals worldwide and tries to capture the complexity of supply chains in synthetic indicators that are comparable across countries. The LPI has provided valuable information for policy makers, traders, and other stakeholders, including researchers and academics, on the role of logistics for growth and the policies needed to support logistics in areas such as infrastructure planning, service provision, and cross-border trade and transport facilitation.

World Bank's LPI analyzes countries in six components:

1. **Customs:** The efficiency of customs and border management clearance.
2. **Infrastructure:** The quality of trade and transport infrastructure.
3. **International Shipment:** The ease of arranging competitively priced shipments.
4. **Logistics Competence:** The competence and quality of logistics services.
5. **Tracking and Tracing:** The ability to track and trace consignments.
6. **Timeliness:** The frequency with which shipments reach consignees within scheduled or expected delivery times.

The components have been chosen based on theoretical and empirical research and on the practical experience of logistics professionals involved in international freight forwarding. LPI uses standard statistical techniques to aggregate the data into a single indicator. This single indicator can be used to compare countries, regions, and income groups. It can also be used for country-level work.

In short, LPI is an interactive benchmarking tool created to help countries identify the challenges and opportunities they face in their performance on trade logistics and what they can do to improve their performance.

9.2.2 Findings of Sixth Edition of LPI Report (2018): Sixth edition of LPI (2018) allows for comparisons across 160 countries. The LPI is based on a worldwide survey of operators on the ground (global freight forwarders and express carriers), providing feedback on the logistics *friendliness* of the countries in which they operate and those with which they trade. They combine in-depth knowledge of the countries in which they operate with informed qualitative assessments of other countries where they trade and experience of global logistics environment. Feedback from operators is supplemented with quantitative data on the performance of key components of the logistics chain in the country of work.

LPI, therefore, consists of both qualitative and quantitative measures and helps build profiles of logistics friendliness for these countries.

Table 9.1 lists top 10 countries of the world in terms of logistics performance. For a comparative view, it also includes the performance of China, India and Pakistan.

Table 9.2 shows trends in LPI ranks of China, India and Pakistan from 2007 through 2018. No pattern is visible in India's rank over the period covered in the table. However, it is clear that in the year 2018, India (with 44th rank) was much below China (with 26th rank). Appropriate measures are, therefore, needed to improve India's rank in LPI.

Improving efficiency of the logistics sector is of high importance for the country's economy as it boosts economic growth, grows exports through global supply chains and generates employment. While India's passenger and freight mobility sectors are becoming more efficient, there are interconnected problems in the system, which need to be addressed to further enhance efficiency.

Logistical inefficiencies lead to reduced employment opportunities, perpetuate a poverty cycle for rural populations, make roads and highways unsafe, and contribute to pollution.

Conversely, enhancing the efficiency of logistics can create high quality economic growth and employment opportunities, improve safety and public health, and support India's successful fulfilment of international commitments towards climate change.

Table 9.1: Logistics Performance Index (LPI) of Top 10 Countries Plus China, India and Pakistan, 2018

Country	LPI rank	LPI score
Germany	1	4.20
Sweden	2	4.06
Belgium	3	4.04
Austria	4	4.03
Japan	5	4.03
Netherlands	6	4.02
Singapore	7	4.00
Denmark	8	3.99
U.K.	9	3.99
Finland	10	3.97
China	**26**	**3.61**
India	**44**	**3.18**
Pakistan	**122**	**2.42**

Source: World Bank, *Trade Logistics in the Global Economy, 2018*.

Table 9.2: Trends in Logistics Performance Index (LPI) Ranks of China, India and Pakistan, 2007 to 2018

Country	2007	2010	2012	2014	2016	2018
China	30	27	26	28	27	26
India	39	47	46	54	35	44
Pakistan	68	110	71	72	68	122

Source: World Bank, *Trade Logistics in the Global Economy, 2007, 2010, 2012, 2014, 2016 and 2018*.

Efficient logistics are a cornerstone for the continuation of India's economic development over the coming decades. The robust growth in manufacturing envisioned through the "Make-in-India" initiative will demand high levels of logistical efficiency, which means that goods must not only be produced, they must also be efficiently transported to markets at reasonable prices.

While the growth in GDP created by logistics improvements is important, even more important is the quality of that growth and the employment and income it creates, especially for the most economically vulnerable segments of the population.

Logistics efficiency can also benefit farmers through reduction in loss and wastage of produce during transportation to markets. Reducing that wastage could both provide an income boost to farmers and also lower overall prices for produce, creating better access to high quality food for Indian citizens.

Furthermore, poor logistics practices often lead to unsafe practices such as overloading of trucks, which compromise road safety both for truck drivers and those with whom they share the road.

Finally, improved logistics can bring about important environmental benefits. Improving the efficiency of logistics can rein in growing demand for trucking services, helping India to meet its international climate commitments while simultaneously reducing pollution in India's most populated cities.

Infrastructure or transport quality is a particular area of concern for the logistics sector. About 35 percent of export-import cargo originates in or is destined for hinterland locations.

As per the document *Strategy for New India @75*, released by NITI Aayog in November 2018, "Indian logistics industry employs more than 22 million people (as of 2016). Between 2011-12 and 2015-16, the logistics sector's value has grown at a compound annual growth rate (CAGR) of 7.8 percent. However, existing logistics costs in India are high relative to other countries. Logistics costs have been estimated at 14 percent of India's GDP relative to 9 percent of GDP in the United States, 11 percent in Japan, 12 percent in Korea and

14.9 percent in China. A 10 percent decrease in indirect logistics cost has the potential to increase exports by 5-8 percent". [1]

9.2.3 Logistics Division in the Department of Commerce: Recognizing its importance for exports and growth, the government has included logistics in the harmonized master list of the infrastructure sub-sector. This will ease access to credit and simplify the approvals process for building infrastructure in the sector.

The Logistics Division in the Department of Commerce, Ministry of Commerce and Industry, Government of India was created on July 7, 2017 consequent to the amendment to the Second Schedule of the Government of India (Allocation of Business) Rules, 1961. It allocated the task of "Integrated Development of Logistics Sector" to the Department of Commerce. The Division is headed by a Special Secretary to Government of India and has been given the mandate to develop an Action Plan for the integrated development of the logistics sector in the country, by way of policy changes, improvement in existing procedures, identification of bottlenecks and gaps and introduction of technology in this sector.

Logistics Division has also planned to create an IT backbone and develop a National Logistics Information Portal which will also be an online logistics market place that will serve to bring together the various stakeholders—logistics service providers, buyers as well as Central and State Government agencies such as customs, Director General of Foreign Trade (DGFT), railways, ports, airports, inland waterways, coastal shipping etc.—on a single platform.

The planned activities of the Logistics Division shall have an impact not only on the domestic movement of goods by bringing down the overall cost and increasing the speed and ease of goods movement, but shall also contribute towards making Indian goods more competitive in the global market. With the improvement in India's ranking in the LPI, Indian exports would automatically see an enhanced growth.

Endnote

1. NITI Aayog, *Strategy for New India @75*, November 2018, p. 85.

10

Skill Development, Innovations and Entrepreneurship

The existence of a dynamic entrepreneurial and managerial class capable of taking risks and dealing with competitive pressure is an important pre-requisite. It also depends upon the quality of public sector managers responsible for investment and productivity in the public sector enterprises.

Growth also depends on the availability of labour in adequate quantities, and with the right kind of skills to support rapid growth. India, for example, has the benefit of a demographic dividend because the age structure of the population ensures that the labour force will be growing in the future. However, the level of skills of the labour force needs to be enhanced.

10.1 Skill Development

India presently faces a dual challenge of paucity of highly trained workforce, as well as non-employability of large sections of the conventionally educated youth, who possess little or no job skills.

Occupational patterns are changing; and new jobs and job titles, job enlargement, job enrichment, and new flexible work arrangements are emerging. Employment demands are shifting towards higher skill categories. It is imperative, therefore, for India to move up the skill-ladder and produce a larger number of people with higher education and generic training for new types of knowledge work, both in high skill services and high technology industrial production. Knowledge professionals will need support from middle-skilled workers in new knowledge and technology areas. The skill development system will need to meet this challenge. The response time is limited as the rate of change is high and accelerating.

10.1.1 National Policy for Skill Development and Entrepreneurship (NPSDE), 2015: The Ministry of Labour and Employment, Government of India, had formulated a National Policy on Skill Development in 2009. The objective of this policy was to empower all individuals through improved skills, knowledge, nationally and internationally recognized qualifications to gain access to decent employment and ensure India's competitiveness in the global market.

On July 15, 2015, Prime Minister Narendra Modi launched the National Policy for Skill Development and Entrepreneurship (NPSDE), 2015 along with the following three other landmark initiatives of the Ministry of Skill Development and Entrepreneurship:

1. National Skill Development Mission (NSDM).
2. Pradhan Mantri Kaushal Vikas Yojana (PMKVY).
3. Skill Loan Scheme.

The 2009 policy was, thus, superseded by NPSDE, 2015. The new policy tries to bring the world of education and training closer to the world of work so as to enable them together build a strong India.

The Ministry of Skill Development and Entrepreneurship, Government of India, is an integral part of the government policy on *Sabka Saath, Sabka Vikaas* and its commitment to overall human resources development to take advantage of the demographic profile of India in the coming years. The objective of NPSDE, 2015 is to meet the challenge of skilling at scale with speed and standard (quality). It aims to provide an umbrella framework to all skilling activities being carried out within the country, and to align them to common standards and link the skilling with demand centres.

In addition to laying down the objectives and expected outcomes, it also identifies the various institutional frameworks which can act as the vehicle to reach the expected outcome. The national policy also provides clarity and coherence on how skill development efforts across the country can be aligned within the existing institutional arrangements. This policy links skills development to improved employability and productivity.

10.1.2 National of Skill India Mission (NSDM): NSDM) was approved by the Union Cabinet on July 1, 2015, and officially launched by the Prime Minister on July 15, 2015 on the occasion of World Youth Skills Day. 18,000 plus ITI graduating students received job offer letters on the occasion of World Youth Skills Day. Government set a target to provide skill training to 40.02 crore people by 2022.

NSDM has been developed to create convergence across sectors and States in terms of skill training activities. Further, to achieve the vision of Skilled India, NSDM would not only consolidate and co-ordinate skilling efforts, but also expedite decision making across sectors to achieve skilling at scale with speed and standards. It will be implemented through a streamlined institutional mechanism driven by Ministry of Skill Development and Entrepreneurship (MSDE).

The Ministry of Skill Development and Entrepreneurship (earlier Department of Skill Development and Entrepreneurship, first created in July 2014) was set up in November 2014 to drive the Skill India agenda in a Mission Mode in order to converge existing skill training initiatives and combine scale and quality of skilling efforts, with speed.

The Ministry, therefore, launched NSDM which will provide the overall institutional framework to rapidly implement and scale up skill development efforts across India. It seeks to provide the institutional capacity to train a minimum of 300 million skilled people by the year 2022.

10.1.3 Pradhan Mantri Kaushal Vikas Yojana (PMKVY): On July 15, 2015, Prime Minister Narendra Modi launched the Pradhan Mantri Kaushal Vikas Yojana (PMKVY), 2015.

The slogan *Kaushal Bharat, Kushal Bharat* suggests that skilling Indians (*Kaushal Bharat*) will result in a happy, healthy, prosperous and strong nation (*Kushal Bharat*).

PMKVY is the flagship, demand-driven, reward-based skill training scheme of the Ministry of Skill Development and Entrepreneurship (MSDE). It is intended to incentivise skill training by providing financial rewards to candidates who successfully complete approved skill training programmes. For the first time, the skills of young people who lack formal certification, such as workers in India's vast unorganised sector, will be recognised. Through an initiative known as recognition of prior learning (RPL), 10 lakh youth will be assessed and certified for the skills that they already possess.

Under PMKVY, skill cards and skill certificates are awarded which allow trainees to share their skill identity with employers. Each skill card and skill certificate features a quick response code (QR Code), which can be read through a QR reader on mobile devices. Trainees can use these to share their skill qualifications with employers in a quick and reliable way during the job search process.

Approved for another four years (2016-2020) to benefit 10 million youth, training and assessment fees under PMKVY are completely paid by the Government.

10.1.4 Udaan: Udaan is a Special Industry Initiative for Jammu and Kashmir (J&K) in the nature of partnership between the corporates of India and Ministry of Home Affairs and implemented by National Skill Development Corporation. The programme aims to provide skills training and enhance the employability of unemployed youth of J&K. The scheme covers graduates, post-graduates and three year engineering diploma holders. It has two objectives:

1. To provide an exposure to the unemployed graduates to the best of Corporate India;
2. To provide Corporate India, an exposure to the rich talent pool available in the State.

The scheme aims to cover 40,000 youth of J&K over a period of 5 years and a sum of ₹ 750 crore has been earmarked for implementation of the scheme over a period of 5 years to cover other incidental expenses such as travel cost, boarding and lodging, stipend and travel and medical insurance cost for the trainees and administration cost. Further corporates are eligible for partial reimbursement of training expense incurred for the candidates who have been offered jobs.

10.1.5 Skill Loan Scheme: Launched on July 15, 2015, the scheme will make available loans ranging from ₹ 5,000-₹ 1.5 lakh to 34 lakh youth of India seeking to attend skill development programmes.

10.1.6 Deen Dayal Upadhyaya Grameen Kaushalya Yojana (DDU-GKY): The Ministry of Rural Development (MoRD), Government of India announced DDU-GKY on September 25, 2014. DDU-GKY is a part of the National Rural Livelihood Mission (NRLM), tasked with the dual objectives of adding diversity to the incomes of rural poor families and cater to the career aspirations of rural youth.

DDU-GKY is uniquely focused on rural youth between the ages of 15 and 35 years from poor families. As a part of the Skill India Campaign, it plays an instrumental role in supporting the social and economic programmes of the Government like Make in India, Digital India, Smart Cities, Start-up India, and Stand-up India campaigns.

National Policy for Skill Development and Entrepreneurship, 2015 has identified a skills gap of 109.73 million in 24 key sectors by the year 2022. This presents an unprecedented opportunity for India to train its youth population and place them in jobs across the world and realize its demographic dividend.

Innovation from partners is encouraged to build scale and capacity. Its unique implementation structure involves partners, who are by nature, committed to changing lives and are experts in their areas. They form a part of the skilling ecosystem integrated by DDU-GKY. Partners are supported through investment, capacity building, strategies for retention, linkages to international placement and technology support for training purposes.

10.2 Innovations

Innovation is a process whereby people or groups of

people with an entrepreneurial mindset (organizations, enterprises) develop new ideas or absorb and adapt existing ones. Together with institutions and policies that affect their behaviour and performance, they create new products, processes, and forms of organization. Innovation is not only about scientists in laboratories, theoretical science, or new discoveries. It is about building the capacity to find solutions to practical everyday development problems. Hence, an innovative economy is marked by ideas for new products or new ways of doing things and transforming them into profitable products or activities.

10.2.1 Atal Innovation Mission (AIM): Finance Minister in his Budget Speech 2015-16 announced the Government's intention to establish the Atal Innovation Mission (AIM) in NITI Aayog and stated that initially a sum of ₹ 150 crore would be earmarked for this purpose. The overarching purpose of this mission is to promote a culture of entrepreneurship and innovation in India. In the years to come, entrepreneurship and innovation are expected to be an ever more important source of growth and job creation. New technology also has the potential to find solutions to pressing economic and social problems. AIM is seen as critical to expediting the entrepreneurial process in India.

10.2.2 Global Innovation Index (GII): GII is published annually since 2007 by World Intellectual Property Organization (WIPO). [1] GII report is compiled by WIPO, Cornell University and other GII knowledge partners. The core of the GII Report consists of a ranking of world economies' innovation capabilities and results. Recognizing the key role of innovation as a driver of economic growth and prosperity, and the need for a broad vision of innovation applicable to developed and emerging economies, the GII includes indicators that go beyond the traditional measures of innovation, such as the level of research and development.

GII is a detailed quantitative tool that helps global decision makers better understand how to stimulate the innovative activity that drives economic and human development. GII is a leading benchmarking tool for business executives, policy makers and others seeking insight into the state of innovation around the world. Policymakers, business leaders and other stakeholders use the GII to evaluate progress on a continual basis.

The twelfth edition of Global Innovation Index was released in July 2019. It ranked 129 economies based on 80 indicators, ranging from intellectual property filing rates to mobile-application creation, education spending and scientific and technical publications. Its 80 indicators explore a broad vision of innovation, including political environment, education, infrastructure and business sophistication.

GII 2018 analyzed the energy innovation landscape of the next decade and identified possible breakthroughs in fields such as energy production, storage, distribution, and consumption. It also looked at how breakthrough innovation occurs at the grassroots level and described how small-scale renewable systems are on the rise. The theme for 2019 was "Creating Healthy Lives: The Future of Medical Innovation".

India, which was ranked 81 in 2015, has steadily improved its ranking in the last four years. It went up to 66th spot in 2016, 60th in 2017, 57th in 2018 and 52nd in 2019. Thus, India jumped 29 notches in four years. The 2019 rankings put China at 14th place and Pakistan at 105 (Table 10.1).

10.2.3 Bloomberg Innovation Index, 2019: Bloomberg is a New York-based media firm. Bloomberg's annual innovation index, now in its seventh year, is framed using dozens of criteria including manufacturing ability, concentration of high technology public organizations, and expenditure on research and development.

The ranking for 2019 was commenced with the involvement of 200 nations. Each was scored on a 0-100 scale. Countries which did not report data were eliminated, trimming the total list to 95. Bloomberg published data for top 60 countries. Top 10 countries plus China and India are shown in Table 10.2.

Table 10.1: Global Innovation Index Rankings, 2019
Top 10 Countries of the World and
China, India and Pakistan

Country	Rank	Score (0-100)
Top Ten Countries of the World		
Switzerland	1 (1)	67.24
Sweden	2 (3)	63.65
United States of America	3 (6)	61.73
Netherlands	4 (2)	61.44
United Kingdom	5 (4)	61.30
Finland	6 (7)	59.83
Denmark	7 (8)	58.44
Singapore	8 (5)	58.37
Germany	9 (9)	58.19
Israel	10 (.)*	57.43
India and its Neighbours		
China	14 (17)	54.82
India	52 (57)	36.58
Pakistan	105 (109)	25.36

Figures in parentheses indicate ranking of the country concerned in 2018.
* Not in top 10 in 2018.
Source: United Nations, World Intellectual Property Organization (WIPO), *Global Innovation Index 2019.*

Table 10.2: Bloomberg Innovation Index Rankings, 2019
Top 10 Countries plus China and India

Rank	Country	Rank	Country
1 (1)	South Korea	7 (2)	Sweden
2 (4)	Germany	8 (11)	USA
3 (7)	Finland	9 (6)	Japan
4 (5)	Switzerland	10 (9)	France
5 (10)	Israel	16 (19)	China
6 (3)	Singapore	54 (debut)*	India

Figures in parentheses show ranks in 2018.
* India entered the list of top 60 countries for the first time.

A. Highlights of the Index: These are as under:

1. South Korea is the most innovative country of 2019.
2. USA grabbed the 8th position.
3. China bagged the 16th position in the annual ranking.
4. United Kingdom fell to 18th position losing two spots to China.
5. World's largest emerging economies including India, Mexico, Saudi Arabia, and Vietnam also made their debut in the annual index.
6. South Africa solely represented Sub-Saharan nation in the listing.

10.2.4 NITI Aayog, India Innovation Index, 2019: NITI Aayog's first ever *India Innovation Index, 2019* was released on October 17, 2019. NITI Aayog, along with the Institute for Competitiveness, released the report with the objective of providing a comprehensive overview of the innovation ecosystem of different administrative units of the country. The index was calculated as the average of scores of its two dimensions: enablers and performance. The report defined the following 5 enablers which act as inputs to the innovation environment: (a) human capital, (b) investment, (c) knowledge employment, (d) business environment and (e) safety and legal environment. The 2 performance pillars are: (a) knowledge output and (b) knowledge diffusion.

The index showed that the innovation ecosystem is strong in southern and western India. Delhi and Haryana are exceptions to this trend.

Karnataka emerged as the most innovative major state in India followed by Tamil Nadu, Maharashtra, Telangana, Haryana and others.

Sikkim took the top spot among north-eastern and hill states. Delhi was placed at the top spot among Union Territories, city and small states (Table 10.3).

Government policy that favours innovation can have significant impact on growth and job creation in the economy, as indicated by economists that show innovation and productivity to be endogenously generated. Furthermore, India has a latent science and engineering talent pool, which may be particularly advantageous. This strength should be capitalised to generate indigenous intellectual capital.

Table 10.3: India Innovation Index: State Level Performance

Major States	**Rank**	**Score**
Karnataka	1	35.65
Tamil Nadu	2	32.98
Maharashtra	3	29.93
Telengana	4	22.06
Haryana	5	20.55
Kerala	6	19.58
Uttar Pradesh	7	19.08
West Bengal	8	18.21
Gujarat	9	16.86
Andhra Pradesh	10	14.51
Punjab	11	13.67
Odisha	12	12.66
Rajasthan	13	11.00
Madhya Pradesh	14	9.70
Chhattisgarh	15	8.06
Bihar	16	7.99
Jharkhand	17	6.20
North-East and Hill States		
Sikkim	1	15.49
Himachal Pradesh	2	13.76
Uttarakhand	3	13.12
Manipur	4	11.69
Jammu & Kashmir	5	11.07
Tripura	6	8.54
Arunachal Pradesh	7	8.50
Assam	8	7.74
Nagaland	9	7.49
Mizoram	10	6.88
Meghalaya	11	6.38

contd...

UTs/City States/Small States		
Delhi	1	42.98
Chandigarh	2	27.97
Goa	3	22.49
Puducherry	4	13.94
A&N Islands	5	12.75
Daman and Diu	6	12.10
Dadra and Nagar Haveli	7	11.74
Lakshadweep	8	8.35

Source: NITI Aayog, India Innovation Index, 2019.

10.3 Entrepreneurship

The growth and prosperity of all economies remains highly dependent on entrepreneurial activity. Entrepreneurs are the essence of economic growth as they provide a source of income and employment for themselves, create employment for others, produce new and innovative products or services, and drive greater upstream and downstream value-chain activities. Supportive environments are increasingly essential to successful entrepreneurship and these are evolving across the world.

The face of entrepreneurship is also changing. Across the world, entrepreneurs are increasingly young and/or female due to increasing unemployment. The public and private sector each have an important role to play in creating entrepreneurial ecosystems that, in addition to funding, are essential to promoting entrepreneurial success.

Highlighting the diversity of the country, four kinds of entrepreneurial activities exist: (a) factor-driven entrepreneurship, (b) efficiency-driven entrepreneurship, (c) innovation-driven entrepreneurship and (d) necessity-driven entrepreneurship.

Developed economies generate entrepreneurial opportunities as a result of their wealth and innovation capacity, yet they also offer more wage employment options to attract those that might otherwise become independent entrepreneurs. If these opportunities for entrepreneurship and innovation are to be captured, it is essential to create an enabling eco-system for entrepreneurship to thrive and instil a mind-set and culture of opportunity and innovation-based motives and entrepreneurial incentives.

Entrepreneurship has been considered the backbone of economic development. It has been well-established that the level of economic growth of a region, to a large extent, depends on the level of entrepreneurial activities in the region. The myth that entrepreneurs are born, no more holds good. Rather, it is well-recognised now that the entrepreneurs can be created and nurtured through appropriate interventions in the form of entrepreneurship development programmes.

In the era of liberalisation, privatisation and globalization along with ongoing IT revolution, capable entrepreneurs are making use of the opportunities emerging from the evolving scenario. However, a large segment of the population, particularly in the industrially backward regions/rural areas generally lags behind in taking advantage of these opportunities. Therefore, there is a need to provide skill development and entrepreneurship development training to such people in order to bring them to mainstream of economic growth.

10.3.1 Self-Employment and Talent Utilisation (SETU): The National Policy for Skill Development and Entrepreneurs envisaged fostering entrepreneurship and grassroots innovation by providing support in terms of fiscal incentives, creation of grassroots technology innovation hubs, legal support and market linkages. The Government has established a mechanism to be known as SETU under NITI Aayog to support all aspects of start-up businesses and other self-employment activities, particularly in technology-driven areas.

As stated in the Budget Speech of the Finance Minister, 2015-16, SETU is to be a Techno-Financial, Incubation and Facilitation Programme to support all aspects of start-up businesses and other self-employment activities, particularly in technology-driven areas. Initially, a sum of ₹ 1,000 crore was set aside for the purpose

NITI Aayog constituted an Expert Committee on Innovation and Entrepreneurship (Chairman: Tarun Khanna) in April 2015 for working out the detailed contours of the Atal Innovation Mission (AIM) and SETU to achieve the stated objectives. The Committee submitted its report in August 2015.

10.3.2 India Aspiration Fund (IAF): In August 2015, Government launched IAF to be set up as a fund of funds under the Small Industries Development Bank of India (SIDBI) in order to boost the start-up ecosystem in the country. An initial corpus of ₹ 400 crore has been already allocated to various venture funds under it. The objective of the IAF is to catalyse tens of thousands of crores of equity investment into start-ups and MSMEs creating employment of lakhs of persons, mostly educated youth, over the next four to five years.

The fund has committed up to ₹ 60 crore in IvyCap Ventures, up to ₹ 30 crore for Blume Ventures and up to ₹ 20 crore for Carpediem Capital Partners.

India is witnessing a start-up revolution and to harness the potential of India's innovators and entrepreneurs a vibrant financial ecosystem is essential. IAF will play a vital role in this financial ecosystem.

This is a well-structured fund and since it is built on sectoral allocation, it will provide investment to start-ups in sectors which are not hot today for venture funds but will become hot in future.

10.3.3 SIDBI Make in India Loan for Small Enterprises (SMILE): SMILE was launched in August 2015. The objective of SMILE scheme is to provide soft loans in the nature of quasi-equity and term loans on relatively soft terms to MSMEs. The loan scheme's focus will be on 25 sectors under Government's Make-in-India programme with emphasis on financing smaller enterprises within the MSME sector.

The Department of Electronics and Information Technology is implementing a scheme entitled 'Technology Incubation and Development of Entrepreneurs' (TIDE) under which 147 start-ups have been supported at 25 TIDE centres established in premier institutes like IITs, NITs, IIMs etc.

Endnote

1. World Intellectual Property Organization (WIPO) is the global forum for intellectual property (IP) policy, services, information and cooperation. A specialized agency of the United Nations, WIPO assists its 191 member states in developing a balanced international IP legal framework to meet society's evolving needs. It provides business services for obtaining IP rights in multiple countries and resolving disputes. It delivers capacity-building programs to help developing countries benefit from using IP. And it provides free access to unique knowledge banks of IP information.

11

Digitization of the Indian Economy

In the modern world, digital networking and communication infrastructures provide a global platform over which people and organizations devise strategies, interact, communicate, collaborate and search for information.

It is widely accepted that the growth of the digital economy has widespread impact on the whole economy. Various attempts at categorising the size of the impact on traditional sectors have been made.

Given its expected broad impact, traditional firms are actively assessing how to respond to the changes brought about by the digital economy. For corporations, timing of their response is of the essence. Banks are trying to innovate and use digital tools to improve their traditional business.

Information technology (IT) sector has made remarkable progress in recent years. It has transformed the world, enabling innovation and enhancing productivity, connecting people and communities, and improving standards of living and providing opportunities across the globe. While changing the way individuals live, interact, and work, IT has also proven to be a key enabler for enhanced competitiveness and economic and societal modernisation, as well as an important instrument for bridging economic and social divides and reducing poverty.

11.1 India and Information Technology (IT) Services

India has emerged in recent years as the most preferred destination for outsourcing of IT services. The vibrant IT industry is contributing immensely by providing information about latest technology and international business practices. IT has been contributing substantially to the economic growth of the country. More importantly, it can immensely help in accelerating the growth momentum by enhancing efficiency, competitiveness and technological edge across sectors, including particularly strategic sectors. Equally significant is the contribution of IT in enabling inclusive growth and development, and in ensuring that people across the length and breadth of the country have access to the opportunities generated by growth.

Differential access to economic opportunities across nations that characterized the past has been fundamentally impacted and altered by IT and telecom. The same phenomenon can be exploited to help equalize access to opportunity within the country, straddling urban and rural, rich and poor. Ubiquitous and reliable connectivity holds the key. IT is thus not just a major part of a better future, but more importantly, is the key instrument in realising it. Imagining a credibly optimistic future and designing IT policy to realize that vision, could therefore be a self-fulfilling prophesy.

The pace of technological advance is accelerating and electronics is increasingly becoming a ubiquitous and intrinsic part of people's behaviours and social networks as well as of business practices and government activities and service provision. These transformations will continue to guide human progress forward by further leveraging IT's positive social, political, and economic impact on government, enterprise, and civil society alike.

India is today a global source of skilled IT manpower. IT permeates all aspects of society, business, governance, finance and indeed every other aspect of modern life. Hence, India's strengths in IT constitute a major strategic advantage that needs to be maintained and systematically nurtured. Existing capabilities are already powerful enough to transform the economy, government and society.

Appropriate application of IT has the potential to vastly improve productivity and efficiency. Therefore, there is a need to promote the use of IT platforms and convergence of technologies to ensure better delivery of public services, increased efficiency in the implementation of the Government's flagship programmes and the overall competitiveness of the economy, since IT applications will have a pervasive effect on the resilience and dynamism of all sectors of the economy.

11.2 World Digital Competitiveness Ranking, 2019

World Digital Competitiveness Ranking is prepared by IMD (International Institute for Management Development) World Competitiveness Centre based in Lausanne (Switzerland). The ranking has relevance to answer the following questions:

1. How prepared are economies to productively use the transformative technologies of our time?
2. Do countries have a feasible framework to facilitate the adoption and use of digitalization?
3. And how ready are they to embrace the implications of digital disruption?

Started in 2017, the ranking measures the capacity and readiness of 63 economies to develop, adopt and explore digital technologies as a key driver for economic transformation in business, government and wider society. The index ranks the countries based on the following three factors:

1. **Knowledge:** The capacity to understand and learn new technologies.
2. **Technology:** The competence to develop new digital innovations.
3. **Future Readiness:** The preparedness for the coming developments.

The first factor, knowledge, refers to the intangible infrastructure, which underlines the process of digital transformation through the discovery, understanding and learning of new technologies.

The technology factor assesses the overall context through which the development of digital technologies is enabled. Technology not only affects how businesses perform but also how economies function and prepare for the future. Governments around the world are investing heavily in their digital economy to enhance value creation and prosperity.

Finally, the future readiness factor which examines the level of preparedness of an economy to assume its digital transformation.

The top 5 countries in the 2019 digital competitiveness index remained the same as in 2018. The US continued to top the rankings list, followed by Singapore, Sweden, Denmark and Switzerland (Table 11.1).

The other countries in the top ten included the Netherlands (6th rank), Finland (7th rank), Hong Kong (8th rank), Norway (9th rank) and South Korea (10th rank) (Table 11.1).

India moved up four places to 44th rank in 2019 as compared to 48th rank in 2018 (Table 11.1). Its position in 2019 improved overall in all factors including knowledge, technology and future readiness in exploring more digital technologies.

Table 11.1: Digital Competitive Ranking, 2019
Top Ten plus China and India

Country	Rank	Score (0-100)
USA	1 (1)	100.00
Singapore	2 (2)	99.37
Sweden	3 (3)	96.07
Denmark	4 (4)	95.22
Switzerland	5 (5)	94.64
Netherlands	6 (9)	94.26
Finland	7 (7)	93.73
Hong Kong	8 (11)	93.68
Norway	9 (6)	93.67
South Korea	10 (14)	91.29
China	22 (30)	84.29
India	44 (48)	64.95

Note: Figures in parentheses indicate 2018 rankings.
Source: IMD World Competitiveness Centre, *World Digital Competitiveness Ranking, 2019*, pp. 26-27.

India's biggest improvement in 2019 was in the technology sub-factor level, where it held the first position in telecommunications investment.

The results of the 2019 ranking showed that top performing countries largely focused on the factors that contribute to the generation of knowledge. Western economies remain as the main digital hubs and leaders as global knowledge centres. Several Asian economies improved this year reducing the digital gap mainly through an advancement in the technology and future readiness factors. However, it seems that they remain dependent of western economies for the generation of knowledge. In addition, the data show that factors related to political stability affect the availability of funding technological development. This is particularly relevant for SMEs in countries with limited political stability.

11.3 India's E-payment Ranking in Global Survey

According to the 2018 survey by The Economist Intelligence Unit, commissioned by payments company Visa, India is taking rapid strides in advancing government e-payments capabilities and is one of the top-performing countries in terms of citizen-to-government (C2G), business-to-government (B2G) and government-to-business (G2B) transactions. The country holds the top ranking on B2G and G2B, and comes third on C2G jointly with Argentina.

In the 73-country survey, India's overall ranking on the government's adoption of e-payments moved up to 28th in 2018, from 36th in 2011.

The survey looks at availability of government electronic transaction services and the underlying environment of mechanisms that support digitization for all transactions in a market, such as policy and infrastructure.

According to the survey, India can further improve its standing by focusing on expanding access to digital infrastructure, investing in socio-economic development, and promoting a healthy, competitive market.

The overall rankings and scores of top ten countries plus India, China and Pakistan are presented in Table 11.2. The overall score is a weighted sum of category scores (on a 0-100 scale where 100 is the most favourable). The overall scores reflect the enabling environment for government e-paymcnts adoption.

Table 11.2: Overall Ranking and Scores of Top Ten Countries Plus India, China and Pakistan

Rank	Country	Score
1.	Norway	89.7
2.	France	89.4
3.	Denmark	88.8
4.	Canada	88.6
5.	Australia	88.1
6.	United Kingdom	87.9
7.	South Korea	87.7
8.	Singapore	87.6
9.	Finland	86.2
10.	Sweden	85.8
28.	India	73.3
48.	China	62.4
64.	Pakistan	47.0

Source: Economist Intelligence Unit, *Government E-payments Adoption Ranking Report, September 2018*, p. 17 (excerpted).

India has a rich diversity of digital payment options. Many of these are interoperable, and work through bank accounts, thus giving the users a lot more choice. However, the costs of digital payments are still an issue, and acceptance infrastructure is not widespread.

Card-based electronic payment systems are well-understood at the global and national level, and find acceptance at stores, as well as for online payments. India has had the presence of international players in the payments space for many years. Recently, an Indian player–National Payments Corporation of India (NPCI)—has also introduced card payments through the RuPay scheme.

Cards are usually issued by banks and can be classified on the basis of their issuance, usage and payment by the card holder.

There are three types of cards: (a) pre-paid cards, (b) debit cards and (c) credit cards.

In recent years, non-card electronic payment systems have become very popular. Advancements in banking technology, progress in mobile banking and innovative technologies to facilitate digital payments have enabled large number of small denomination transactions to be handled smoothly in electronic mode. The Government of India has taken policy decisions to encourage cashless/electronic transactions. Non-card electronic payment modes include the following:

1. Real Time Gross Settlement (RTGS).
2. National Electronic Funds Transfer (NEFT).
3. Electronic Clearing Services (ECS).
4. Immediate Payment Services (IMPS).
5. Unified Payments Interface (UPI).
6. Unstructured Supplementary Service Data (USSD).
7. Aadhaar-enabled Payment System (AEPS).
8. Aadhaar Payment Bridge System (APBS).
9. Bharat Interface for Money (BHIM).
10. BHIM Aadhaar (Only for Merchants).
11. Digital Wallet or Electronic Wallet (E-Wallet).
12. Electronic Toll Collections.

11.4 Digital Transactions: India versus Other Countries

Magnitude of digital transactions in a country can be measured by the number of digital transactions per capita per annum. Annual cashless transactions per capita for select countries are shown in Table 11.3.

Trends in cashless transactions per capita per year in India in recent years are shown in Table 11.4.

Digital payments are an important means of economic development and achieving financial inclusion. The task of deepening digital payments is onerous but not insurmountable. It requires concerted effort of all the stake holders to work together with the aim of achieving a digitally included society.

Reserve Bank of India (RBI) has been taking many

initiatives for encouraging digitisation of payments in the country. Significant inroads have been made in making available a variety of digital payment options and with time their usage has increased. RBI also publishes, from time-to-time, its Vision Document for Payment and Settlement Systems in India, the last being released in May 2019 for the period 2019-21.

Table 11.3: Cashless Transactions Per Capita in Select Countries

S. No.	Country	Number of cashless transaction per capita in 2017
1.	Singapore	782.4
2.	Sweden	497.9
3.	USA	473.6
4.	Euro Area	186.8
5.	Russia	178.5
6.	Brazil	148.5
7.	China	96.7
8.	South Africa	79.2
9.	Indonesia	34.0
10.	India	10.73

Source: Reserve Bank of India, *Report of the High-Level Committee on Deepening of Digital Payments* (Chairman: Nandan Nilekani), May 2019, pp. 22-23.

Table 11.4: Trends in Cashless Transactions Per Capita Per Year in India in Recent Years

Year →	2014	2015	2016	2017	2018	2019	2021
Number of cashless transaction	2.38	4.06	5.44	10.73	13.15	22.42	220.00 Estimated

Source: Reserve Bank of India, *Report of the High-Level Committee on Deepening of Digital Payments* (Chairman: Nandan Nilekani), May 2019, p. 23.

In recent years, Government of India and RBI have set up

various committees for understanding the needs of the payments eco-system and suggesting suitable measures for enhancing the penetration and usage of digital payments.

In order to ensure consistency, and accuracy of data disseminated to the public, it is essential that all data should be available through a single source. This data must be a by-product of the transaction and not be forced for the purpose of measurements.

Hence, High-Level Committee on Deepening of Digital Payments (Chairman: Nandan Nilekani) recommended that, "RBI should be the single source of accurate and complete information for digital payments data for India. RBI may rationalize digital payments definition for better tracking and include all information that can be captured accurately. It may include unregulated sources where possible. RBI should start publishing data on mobile banking and internet banking along with the split of inter-bank and intra-bank transactions, as these services are provided by banks to facilitate payments". [1]

11.5 Cyber Security

Cyber space is a complex environment consisting of interactions among people, software services, devices, networks and worldwide distribution of information and communication technology (ICT).

Owing to the numerous benefits brought about by technological advancements, the cyber space is a common pool used by citizens, businesses, critical information infrastructure, military and governments in a manner that makes it difficult to draw clear boundaries among these different groups. The cyber space is expected to be more complex in the foreseeable future, with many-fold increase in networks and devices connected to it.

One of the biggest attractions of cyber space, as an electronic medium, is its openness and freedom. It is a public domain and there is no restriction on who can use it as long as one adheres to its technical parameters. This has also given rise to concerns over the security of data and information and privacy.

Cyber space is vulnerable to a wide variety of incidents, whether intentional or accidental, man-made or natural, and the data exchanged in the cyber space can be exploited for nefarious purposes by both nation-states and non-state actors.

Cyber attacks and threats are faced by individuals, businesses and governments. These can take the following forms: (a) phishing, (b) hacking, (c) scamming, (d) sniffing, (e) spoofing and (f) denial of service attack.

The only way to protect ourselves from such activities is to be vigilant about our data and protect the data from getting into the hands of scamsters and fraudsters.

Consequences of cyber attacks are disastrous. Large-scale cyber incidents may overwhelm the government, public and private sector resources and services by disrupting functioning of critical information systems. Complications from disruption of such a magnitude may threaten lives, economy and national security.

Openness and freedom of use of the cyber space has given rise to concerns over the security of data and information and privacy. These concerns are common to any network including closed user group networks. However, over the internet, the dimensions of risk are larger while the control measures are relatively fewer.

Rapid identification, information exchange, investigation and co-ordinated response and remediation can mitigate the damage caused by malicious cyber space activity.

Cyber security is a matter of great concern. Although the Government of India and the Telecom Regulatory Authority of India (TRAI) keep coming up with ways to combat cyber crimes, the number of cyber crimes is growing. The Indian Government is reinforcing systems and establishing a centre for cyber security.

To improve customer confidence in digital payments, it is of utmost importance to keep a control on the number of frauds that occur, and to ensure that customers are not impacted. The RBI has already made rules to limit the liability of customers in the event of fraud. Further, the various banks track fraud in the system, and report it to the RBI. Prima facie, the fraud rates in India appear to be low. Regulation has played a key role in this achievement, and it is felt that the requirements of an additional factor of authentication have helped.

Endnote

1. Reserve Bank of India, *Report of the High-Level Committee on Deepening of Digital Payments* (Chairman: Nandan Nilekani), May 2019, p. 21.

12

India's Social Security Net

Social security refers to public assistance in all cases of underserved want. It provides human security to the poor and the destitute.

The social security situation in India is characterised by ambiguity in policy and responsibility. There is a variety of schemes but these have been framed at various points of time and, therefore, do not conform to any overall design reflecting a comprehensive and consistent policy or direction.

The pattern of economic development in India since Independence in 1947 has left in its trail a variety of inequalities which have caused socio-politico tensions. While the economy has performed well in terms of growth rate of gross domestic product (GDP), its performance in terms of human development indicators has been unsatisfactory.

India's recent economic growth performance has, indeed, been creditable. However, such growth must make a demonstrable difference to the lives of the poorest and most vulnerable citizens. India has the potential and the means to secure a reasonable standard of living for all of its citizens. The socio-economically disadvantaged—particularly women in rural areas—are yet to benefit from development efforts.

12.1 Global Hunger Index (GHI), 2019 and India

12.1.1 What is GHI: GHI Report, 2019 was prepared jointly by Concern Worldwide, an Irish aid agency, and Welt Hunger Hilfe, a German organisation.

GHI is a tool designed to comprehensively measure and track hunger at global, regional, and national levels. GHI scores are calculated each year to assess progress and setbacks in combating hunger. The GHI is designed to raise awareness and understanding of the struggle against hunger, provide a way to compare levels of hunger between countries and regions, and call attention to those areas of the world where hunger levels are highest and where the need for additional efforts to eliminate hunger is greatest.

GHI ranks countries on a 100-point scale, with 0 being the best score (no hunger) and 100 being the worst. Values less than 10 reflect low hunger, values from 20 to 34.9 indicate serious hunger, values from 35 to 49.9 are alarming and values of 50 or more are extremely alarming.

GHI calculates the levels of hunger and under-nutrition worldwide. The four indicators for the index are: (a) under-nourishment, (b) child stunting, (c) child wasting (low weight for height) and (d) child mortality.

Commitment to reach Zero Hunger by 2030 is a fundamental ambition of the Sustainable Development Goals.

The Report warned that climate change was causing alarming levels of hunger and making it more difficult to feed people in the world's most vulnerable regions.

17 countries which had a score of less than five (that is their levels of hunger were very low) were not given individual ranks but were ranked collectively (Table 12.1).

Table 12.1 also shows the ranks and scores achieved by China, Sri Lanka, Nepal, Bangladesh, Pakistan and India. The country with the severest problem of hunger at rank 117 with a score of 53.6 was the Central African Republic.

12.1.2 GHI and India: India was classified as a country with *serious* levels of hunger according to the GHI, 2019. India was ranked 102 out of 117 countries in terms of severity of hunger.

India slipped from 95th rank in 2010 to 102nd in 2019 on GHI. In 2000, India's rank was 83rd out of 113 countries.

India's 102nd rank in 2019 meant that there were only 15 other countries in this index which were worse-off than India. Nearly all these were African countries: Sierra Leone,

Uganda, Djibouti, Congo, Sudan, Afghanistan, Zimbabwe, Timor-Leste, Haiti, Liberia, Zambia, Madagascar, Chad, Yemen and Central African Republic.

Table 12.1: Global Hunger Index (GHI) Ranks and Scores of Select Countries, 2019

The following 17 countries which had a score of less than five (i.e. their levels of hunger were very low) were not given individual ranks but were ranked collectively: Belarus, Bosnia & Herzegovina, Bulgaria, Chile, Costa Rica, Croatia, Cuba, Estonia, Kuwait, Latvia, Lithuania, Montenegro, Romania, Slovak Republic, Turkey, Ukraine and Uruguay		
Country	**Rank**	**Score**
China	25	6.5
Sri Lanka	66	17.1
Nepal	73	20.8
Bangladesh	88	25.8
Pakistan	94	28.5
India	102	30.3
Central African Republic	117	53.6

Source: Global Hunger Index, 2019.

The poor performance of the country between 2010 and 2019 was attributed mainly to the increase in prevalence of wasting among children under five. Child wasting in India was the highest rate of wasting for any country in the Report at 20.8 percent. Even conflict-ridden Yemen and climate crisis-hit Djibouti fared better than India on that front. According to the Report, just 9.6 percent of all children in India between 6 and 23 months of age are fed a minimum acceptable diet.

It is noteworthy that the official National Family Health Survey of 2015-16 also put the prevalence of wasting in India at 21 percent. Gujarat, Jharkhand, Karnataka, Madhya Pradesh, and Maharashtra were the big states that contributed to the high wasting percentage in the country.

However, there was an improvement in India's GHI score. The improvement from 38.9 in 2005 to 32 in 2010 was followed by a change from 32 to 30.3 between 2010 and 2019. India demonstrated an improvement in indicators such as under-5 mortality rate, prevalence of stunting among children, and prevalence of under-nourishment owing to inadequate food.

The report made a mention of the Swachh Bharat campaign but said that it had not worked well enough, despite being important: "Even with new latrine construction, however, open defecation is still practiced. This situation jeopardizes the population's health and consequently, children's growth and development as their ability to absorb nutrients is compromised".

12.1.3 Definitions:

A. Hunger: The problem of hunger is complex, and different terms are used to describe its various forms. Hunger is usually understood to refer to the distress associated with a lack of sufficient calories. The Food and Agriculture Organization of the United Nations (FAO) defines food deprivation, or under-nourishment, as the consumption of too few calories to provide the minimum amount of dietary energy that each individual requires to live a healthy and productive life, given that person's sex, age, stature, and physical activity level.

B. Under-nutrition: Under-nutrition goes beyond calories and signifies deficiencies in any or all of the following: energy, protein, and/or essential vitamins and minerals. Under-nutrition is the result of inadequate intake of food in terms of either quantity or quality, poor utilization of nutrients due to infections or other illnesses, or a combination of these immediate causes. These, in turn, are caused by a range of underlying factors, including household food insecurity; inadequate maternal health or childcare practices; or inadequate access to health services, safe water, and sanitation.

C. Malnutrition: Malnutrition refers more broadly to both under-nutrition (problems caused by deficiencies) and over-nutrition (problems caused by unbalanced diets, such as consuming too many calories in relation to requirements with or without low intake of micronutrient-rich foods).

D. Over-nutrition: Over-nutrition, resulting in overweight, obesity, and non-communicable diseases, is becoming increasingly common throughout the world, with implications for human health, government expenditures, and food systems development. While over-nutrition is an important concern, the GHI focuses specifically on issues relating to under-nutrition.

12.2 Three-tier Universal Security System for the Poor

Development and empowerment of scheduled castes (SCs), scheduled tribes (STs), other backward classes (OBCs), minorities, disabled and other social groups in order to bring them at par with the rest of society is a commitment enshrined in the Constitution. Policies of the Central and State Governments have tried to ensure equal rights, and access to benefits and resources to disadvantaged groups in society to enable them to develop their potential and capacities as agents of social change.

Encouraged by the success of the Pradhan Mantri Jan Dhan Yojana, the Government of India proposed to work towards creating a universal social security system for all Indians, specially the poor and the under-privileged and the workers in the unorganised sector, using the bank accounts as the basis for launching the schemes.

Jan Dhan Yojana ensures universal banking coverage across all the six lakh villages of the country, by providing at least one Basic Banking Account, per household. It provides all households in the country, both rural and urban, access to multiple financial services like bank account with RuPay debit card, access to credit, remittance, insurance and pension. Thus, the mission not only brought the excluded sections from the society into the financial mainstream but made the transfer of benefits of various subsidy schemes of the government more efficient. It was the first step to bring in economic equality and remove financial untouchability.

In order to achieve the goal of universal social security

system, especially for the poor and the under-privileged, the three-tier social security schemes, announced in the 2015-16 budget, have spread the safety net of protection to people in all strata of life against deprivation and uncertainties. They are the steps towards ensuring financial security and long-term sustenance to families when the earning family member retires, dies or suffers full or partial disability.

A large portion of India's population had been living without any kind of health, accidental, or life insurance for so long. It was estimated that the unorganised sector workers, which constitute 88 percent of the total labour force of 47.29 crore, as per the 66th Round of NSSO Survey of 2011-12, did not have any formal pension provision. The Budget 2015-16 highlighted this issue and proposed the following three social security schemes:

1. Pradhan Mantri Suraksha Bima Yojna.
2. Pradhan Mantri Jeevan Jyoti Bima Yojana.
3. Atal Pension Yojana.

Prime Minister launched the three social security schemes on May 9, 2015. These three schemes are based on Jan Dhan Yojana platform to protect poor and underprivileged citizens at the time of illness, accidents or old age.

12.3 LPG and Kerosene for the Poor

Till recently, the poor in India had limited access to liquefied petroleum gas (LPG), commonly called cooking gas. The spread of LPG cylinders was predominantly in the urban and semi-urban areas with the coverage mostly in middle class and affluent households. The poor had to rely on firewood, coal, dung cakes etc. as primary source of cooking. The smoke from burning such fuels caused alarming household pollution and adversely affected the health of women and children, causing several respiratory diseases/disorders. In addition, women and children had to go through the drudgery of collecting firewood.

Unclean cooking fuels led to premature deaths due to non-communicable diseases such as heart disease, stroke, chronic obstructive pulmonary disease and lung cancer. Indoor air pollution is also responsible for a significant number of acute respiratory illnesses in young children. According to World Health Organization (WHO), smoke inhaled by women from unclean fuel is equivalent to burning 400 cigarettes in an hour.

12.3.1 Pradhan Mantri Ujjwala Yojana (PMUY): PMUY was launched by Prime Minister Narendra Modi on May 1, 2016 in Ballia, Uttar Pradesh. Under this scheme, LPG connections are provided to below poverty line (BPL) families with a support of ₹ 1,600 per connection. Ensuring women's empowerment, especially in rural India, the connections is issued in the name of women of the households. Identification of the BPL families will be done through socio-economic caste census data.

PMUY aims to safeguard the health of women and children by providing them with a clean cooking fuel (LPG), so that they do not have to compromise their health in smoky kitchens or wander in unsafe areas collecting firewood.

12.3.2 PAHAL: Direct Benefit Transfer for LPG Consumer (DBTL) Scheme: Government, as a measure of good governance, has introduced well-targeted system of subsidy delivery to LPG consumers through PAHAL. This initiative of the Government is aimed at rationalizing subsidies to cut subsidy leakages, but not subsidies themselves. PAHAL has entered into Guinness Book of World Records, being the largest Direct Benefit Transfer Scheme.

Every household in the country is entitled to 12 LPG cylinders of 14.2 kg. each at subsidised rates in a year. The amount of subsidy is transferred directly in bank accounts of beneficiaries as a part of extension of Direct Benefit Transfer (DBT) scheme. Any requirement beyond that is to be purchased at market price (non-subsidised LPG rates).

PAHAL has helped in identifying ghost/multiple/inactive accounts. Blocking of such accounts has resulted in considerable savings on the part of Government. Further, Government has taken steps to rationalise the subsidy outgo by excluding such

LPG consumers or his/her spouse having taxable income of above ₹ 10 lakh, from availing LPG subsidy.

12.3.3 Direct Transfer of Cash Subsidy on Public Distribution System (PDS) Kerosene: The Centre allocates subsidised kerosene to the States and Union Territories as affordable cooking fuel for domestic use, mainly to those living below the poverty line.

The Ministry of Oil and Natural Gas has introduced Direct Benefit Transfer through which subsidy is transferred directly to the bank accounts of the beneficiaries, who purchase PDS kerosene at non-subsidised rate. The Aadhaar card has been made mandatory for government subsidy on purchase of kerosene.

Implementation of the scheme is expected to result in better subsidy management through direct transfer of subsidy into bank accounts of beneficiaries. This would result in reducing expenditure on subsidy and also help in curbing diversion of subsidized kerosene.

However, States and Union Territories are encouraged to become *kerosene free* by bringing all households under LPG.

12.4 Mahatma Gandhi National Rural Employment Guarantee Scheme (MGNREGS)

The objective of the MGNREGS is to enhance the livelihood security of unorganised workers in rural areas by guaranteeing 100 days of wage employment in a financial year to a rural household whose members volunteer to do unskilled manual work. The scheme further aims at creating durable assets and strengthening the livelihood resource base of the rural poor.

The significance of MGNREGS lies in the fact that it creates a right-based framework for wage employment programmes and makes the Government legally bound to provide employment to those who seek it. In this way it goes beyond providing a social safety net, and guarantees the right to employment. By prioritizing natural resource management and emphasizing the creation of durable assets it holds the potential of becoming a growth engine for sustainable development of an agriculture-based economy.

MGNREGS has emerged as the backbone of rural income for the poor. It guarantees 100 days of work for one person in a year. The wage rate is ₹ 202 per day. There are demands to increase this limit to 150 days.

12.5 Pradhan Mantri Garib Kalyan Rojgar Abhiyan.

On June 20, 2020, Prime Minister Narendra Modi launched a ₹ 50,000 crore rural jobs programme named as Pradhan Mantri Garib Kalyan Rojgar Abhiyan. It is aimed at creating livelihoods for jobless migrant workers who moved back from the cities to their home villages during the lockdown imposed to stop the spread of coronavirus pandemic.

This initiative will offer 125 days of employment in 116 districts across six states which witnessed large scale reverse migration of workers from the cities, triggering a livelihood crisis. The six states are Bihar, Uttar Pradesh, Madhya Pradesh, Rajasthan, Jharkhand and Odisha.

12.6 Direct Benefit Transfer (DBT) Programme

To bring a paradigm shift in the delivery of services to the citizens, particularly common man and the under-privileged section of society of the country, the Government took a decision to start the DBT programme.

Technology-driven DBT is designed to improve targeting, reduce corruption, eliminate waste, control expenditure, and facilitate reforms. Transfers that were taking place through paper and cash mode are now done through electronic transfers. This has been enabled by rapid roll out of Aadhar (Unique Identity). DBT in tandem with such unique identification has ensured that the benefits reach the target groups faster and minimize inclusion and exclusion errors as well as corruption that are associated with manual processes.

All public sector banks (PSBs) and regional rural banks

(RRBs) have made provision so that the data collected by the Departments/Ministries/Implementing agency concerned can be used for seeding the bank account details in the core banking system (CBS) of banks with Aadhaar. All PSBs have also joined the Aadhaar Payment Bridge of the National Payment Corporation of India for smooth transfer of benefits.

Thus, benefits such as scholarships, pensions, and MGNREGS (Mahatma Gandhi National Rural Employment Guarantee Scheme) wages are directly credited to the bank or post office accounts of identified beneficiaries.

13

Role of Government in the Changed Scenario

The policy of liberalization, privatization and openness has a bearing on the economic role of Central and State Governments in India. It is now generally recognized that government in the past tended to take on too many responsibilities, imposing severe strains on its limited financial and administrative capabilities and also stifling individual initiative. This is not to say that government has no role to play, or only a minimalist role, in promoting development.

On the contrary, Government has a very important role indeed, but a different one from that envisaged in the past. There are many areas, e.g. the social sectors, where its role will clearly have to expand. There are other areas, such as infrastructure development, where gaps are large and the private sector cannot be expected to step in significantly. In these areas, the role of Government may have to be expanded and restructured. It will have to expand in some areas of infrastructure development which are unlikely to attract private investment, e.g. rural infrastructure and road development. In others, e.g. telecommunications, power, ports, etc., the private sector can play a much greater role, provided an appropriate policy framework is in place. Here, the role of the Government needs to change to facilitate such investment as much as possible while still remaining a public sector service provider for quite some time. In all these areas, the role of the government as a regulator ensuring a fair deal for consumers, transparency and accountability, and a level playing field is also extremely important.

13.1 Lessons from Financial Crises of 2008

The failure of Lehman Brothers in mid-September 2008

was followed in quick succession by several other large financial institutions coming under severe stress. This made financial markets around the world uncertain and unsettled. This contagion spread to emerging economies and to India also.

By the middle of September 2008, it became apparent that the global credit crisis had deepened and key financial institutions were in need of help. Governments and central banks across the world, including India, started intervening to cut interest rates, inject liquidity and recapitalize weakening banks and financial institutions. The scale of intervention—through the various bailouts and other fiscal and monetary measures—was unparalleled in the history of the global financial system.

13.1.1 Policy Response to Global Crisis by India: The global economic crisis started impacting India from the beginning of 2008. Rising crude prices, along with the global food grain shortage, caused a spill over into the real economy. As inflation rose, India was forced to repeatedly tighten credit and money supply.

Both the Government of India and Reserve Bank of India (RBI) responded to the challenge in close coordination and consultation. The main plank of the government response was fiscal stimulus while RBI's action comprised monetary accommodation and counter-cyclical regulatory measures. Securities and Exchange Board of India (SEBI) also took some measures to contain the knock-on effects of the crisis.

To counter the negative fallout of the global slowdown on the economy, Indian Government took prompt action by providing substantial fiscal stimulus. Two packages announced on December 7, 2008 and January 2, 2009, provided tax relief to boost demand and aimed at increasing expenditure on public projects to create employment and public assets. These fiscal stimulus packages, together amounting to about 3 percent of GDP, included additional public spending, government guaranteed funds for infrastructure spending, cuts in indirect taxes, expanded guarantee cover for credit to micro and small enterprises, and additional support to exporters. These stimulus packages came on top of an already announced expanded safety net for rural poor, a farm loan waiver package and salary increases for government staff, all of which were expected to stimulate demand.

In addition to expanding public sector investment in infrastructure, Government also took steps to encourage private investment in infrastructure through public-private-partnership (PPP). To ensure that such projects did not face financing difficulties arising from the crisis, arrangements were made to provide refinance to the banks for long-term credit extended to these projects.

Government also announced specific measures to address the impact of global slowdown on India's exports. These included extension of export credit for labour-intensive exports, improving the pre- and post-shipment credit availability, additional allocations for refund of terminal excise duty/Central sales tax and export incentive schemes, and removal of export duty and export ban on certain items. A Committee of Secretaries was set up to address, on continuing basis, procedural problems being faced by exporters.

13.2 Fiscal Deficit is not a Sacred Cow

In the 2020-21 budget, fiscal deficit was shown at a figure of ₹ 7,96,337 crore, which was 3.5 percent of GDP.

Fiscal deficit [1] should not be a matter of concern under all circumstances. Taking clue from Keynesian economics, it is argued that fiscal deficits would be inflationary only if the economy is at full employment or is characterised by supply constraints in certain crucial sectors. If the economy is buoyant, marked by excess industrial capacity, large food stocks, enormous foreign exchange reserves, and low/moderate inflation, a high dose of fiscal deficit is not only non-inflationary, but virtuous for sustaining high growth rate.

Lack of jobs, incomes and hence demand in the wake of

COVID-19 clearly indicates the need for increased public and private spending. Accordingly, the Central Government should invoke the emergency provisions of the Fiscal Responsibility and Budget Management (FRBM) Act to seek relaxation from the fiscal targets as was done to counter the effects of global financial crisis of 2008.

Magnitude, timing, and consequences of fiscal deficit are all related to the prevailing circumstances and requirements of the economy. Extraordinary economic circumstances require extraordinary measures. Government should relax the FRBM targets in order to provide much needed demand boost to counter the situation created by Covid-induced current downturn. The fiscal consolidation process has to be put on hold temporarily. A fiscal stimulus in a year of stress on the macro economy is in line with international best practices.

However, there is a policy dilemma between growth and inflation. Government cannot spend recklessly to boost the economy because that can lead to price rise. A trade-off between growth and inflation is needed. There should not be a panic reaction but a sombre response.

13.3 Effective Public-Private Dialogue

Global experience shows that the best way to ensure reform is being felt is to engage the private sector throughout the reform process. Public-private dialogue platforms are becoming increasingly more popular globally as mechanisms to better inform the business reform initiatives of governments. Institutionalizing a process of dialogue with the private sector enables the government to benefit from feedback in a more systematic manner, by allowing the reform agenda to be jointly prioritized, sequenced and focused so that the reforms are of benefit to business, and are targeted at their biggest constraints. Such platforms enable governments to benefit by implementing reforms that are powerful and are backed by evidence and demand, and simultaneously build effective bridges, working relationships and trust into the reform process.

Action on the outputs of the dialogue process will entail extensive work on either dealing with government processes, or on tackling the underlying way in which governments make and enforcc rules and regulations.

Reaching every Indian directly, with an assurance of the identity of the individual and with the ability to transact financially is now an imperative for both the Government and the private sector alike. The mobile phone, with the level of coverage achieved, is the obvious choice as the preferred device to serve as the front end for this purpose. This would eliminate needless duplication in the form of a variety of smart cards proliferating for purposes ranging from identity to entitlements to financial transactions. Such a scenario not only adds costs and inefficiencies but, even more alarmingly, leads to non-standardized technological islands that cannot later be integrated. Hence, a major policy objective should be to reposition the mobile phone from a mere communication device to an instrument of empowerment that combines communication with proof of identity, fully secure financial and other transaction capability, multi-lingual services and a whole range of other capabilities that ride on them and transcend the literacy barrier.

13.4 Electronics: A Grey Area

Of the triad of telecom, IT and electronics, the last one is the lagging sector and therefore presents special challenges. Billions of dollars are spent every year on importing electronics items. With burgeoning demand fuelled by rising prosperity and no significant increase in domestic output, imports are bound to grow.

Lack of a strong base, an adverse international environment and failure to build an enabling eco-system are among the major barriers. A stage has now been reached where not only the lofty aspirations for the future, but even sustaining growth trends in IT and telecom is critically dependent on India's ability to foster a strong Electronics

Systems Design and Manufacturing (ESDM) base in the country. A holistic view alone can overcome the enormous challenges and help emulate the successes of IT and telecom in electronics. It is in this context that a combination of three interdependent and synergistic policies for IT, telecom and electronics is necessary.

Security of telecom infrastructure is also threatened by a heavy reliance on imported equipment. Given the all-pervasive nature of electronics in a modern economy and its status as a meta sector, absence of substantial manufacturing base also poses severe long-term threats to India's strategic sectors and interests as well as to cyber security, which is a cause for rising concern. However, the silver lining is the strong design and substantial R&D capability that has developed in the country. Fragile power supply situation and low paying capacity, especially in rural areas, underline the need for innovative design, green technology and frugal engineering to create a whole range of new designs and products that are optimized for Indian needs and pockets. Nano technology holds much promise in this respect. The lack of wafer fab facilities in the country, indigenously designed chips and a meaningful electronics component base are gaping holes in India's foundation in the sector.

The Indian IT industry has steadily moved up the value chain and is now fully capable of envisioning and developing a whole range of value added services that can be delivered through computers, mobile phones or other devices. The industry can create and sustain a service delivery platform for such services thereby extending the global reach of the entire service industry. The advent of cloud computing technology has thrown up another wide range of possibilities for India. Indian companies have already begun creating new products and services incorporating their own IPs and patents. The stage is now set for a quantum jump in this trend. Another positive aspect is that there is a growing trend of entrepreneurship and product/service innovation.

Right to Information legislation has led to increased demand for information and transparency which can only be met through effective leveraging of technology.

13.5 Empowerment of Marginalised Groups

The vision of inclusiveness must go beyond the traditional objective of poverty alleviation to encompass equality of opportunity, as well as economic and social mobility for all sections of society, with affirmative action for scheduled castes (SCs), scheduled tribes (STs), other backward classes (OBCs), minorities and women. There must be equality of opportunity to all with freedom and dignity and without social or political obstacles. This must be accompanied by an expansion in the opportunities for economic and social advancement. In particular, individuals belonging to disadvantaged groups should be provided special opportunities to develop their skills and participate in the growth process. This can be ensured only if there is a degree of empowerment that creates the true feeling of participation so necessary in a democratic polity.

Empowerment of disadvantaged and hitherto marginalized groups is, therefore, an essential part of any vision of inclusive growth. India's democratic polity—with the establishment of the third layer of democracy at the panchayati raj level—provides opportunities for empowerment and participation of all groups with reservations for SCs, STs and women. These institutions should be made more effective through greater delegation of power and responsibility to the local level.

Some of the important social problems like poverty, ignorance, over-population and rural backwardness are of a general nature and they are influenced—in varying degree—by factors like squalor and bad housing, malnutrition and physical ill-health, family disorganisation and low standard of living. For a long time, society has remained apathetic to these conditions, but with the awakening of political consciousness and the enthusiasm of organisations and workers to improve social conditions, there is a possibility of developing programmes which could gradually remedy the present situation.

Women belonging to SCs and STs are in a far worse situation by all development indicators. Poverty and deprivation affect them more adversely. Although they work along with men, they are not recognised as producers in their own right. The strategy for the development of SCs and STs will have to include a major thrust for the benefit of womenfolk.

13.6 Governance and Corruption Perceptions Index (CPI), 2018

The World Bank defines governance as "the manner in which power is exercised in the management of a country's economic and social resources for development".

Better governance is crucial for translating the large development and welfare expenditure of the public authorities into enduring outcomes on the ground. While there is general appreciation that development programmes have the right objectives, their implementation on the ground is poor. Implementation of programmes can be improved through a multi-faceted approach relying on professionalization of public service delivery, total quality management (TQM), innovative use of digital and other technologies which improve monitoring and supervision. It can also be improved through: (a) greater emphasis on social mobilisation and capacity building, (b) strengthening of local institutions and (c) building deeper partnerships with civil society organisations and the community to determine the needs and aspirations of the people.

Corruption distorts the decision-making mechanism and leads to an inefficient distribution of resources. Improving anti-corruption efforts is one of the highest rated priorities of the business leaders. India should work closely with the relevant international organizations and give particular importance to the fight against corruption in the public and private sectors. Measures to increase transparency in government-business relations will have a corrective impact on corruption.

13.6.1 Corruption Perceptions Index (CPI), 2018: CPI is an index published annually by Transparency International since 1995 which ranks countries by their perceived levels of public sector corruption, as determined by expert assessments and opinion surveys. CPI scores countries on how corrupt their governments are believed to be.

Transparency International is a non-profit organization that seeks to stop bribery and other forms of public corruption. It is the global civil society organization leading the fight against corruption for the last 25 years.

The purpose of CPI is to take action to combat global corruption with civil societal anti-corruption measures and to prevent criminal activities arising from corruption. Since its inception in 1995, CPI, a flagship research product of Transparency International, has become the leading global indicator of public sector corruption. The index offers an annual snapshot of the relative degree of corruption by ranking countries and territories from all over the globe. In 2012, Transparency International revised the methodology used to construct the index to allow for comparison of scores from one year to the next.

The 2018 CPI draws on 13 surveys and expert assessments to measure public sector corruption in 180 countries and territories, giving each a score from zero (highly corrupt) to 100 (very clean).

Decrease in ratings reflects the deterioration of rule of law and democratic institutions, as well as a rapidly shrinking space for civil society and independent media, in those countries.

A. Highlights of 2018 Index: These are as under:

1. Denmark and New Zealand top the Index with 88 and 87 points, respectively.
2. Somalia, South Sudan, and Syria are at the bottom of the

index, with 10, 13 and 13 points, respectively.

3. The highest scoring region is Western Europe and the European Union, with an average score of 66.
4. The lowest scoring regions are Sub-Saharan Africa (average score 32) and Eastern Europe and Central Asia (average score 35).
5. More than two-thirds of countries scored below 50, with an average score of just 43. It reveals continued failure of most countries to significantly control corruption.
6. Despite some progress, most countries are failing to make serious inroads against corruption.
7. With many democratic institutions under threat across the globe, often by leaders with authoritarian or populist tendencies, there is need to do more to strengthen checks and balances and protect citizens' rights.
8. Cross analysis with global democracy data reveals a link between corruption and the health of democracies. Full democracies score an average of 75 on the CPI; flawed democracies score an average of 49; hybrid regimes, which show elements of autocratic tendencies, score 35; autocratic regimes perform worst, with an average score of just 30 on the CPI.

B. Remedies: To make real progress against corruption and strengthen democracy around the world, Transparency International calls on all governments to:

1. Strengthen the institutions responsible for maintaining checks and balances over political power, and ensure their ability to operate without intimidation.
2. Close the implementation gap between anti-corruption legislation, practice and enforcement.
3. Support civil society organisations which enhance political engagement and public oversight over government spending, particularly at the local level.
4. Support a free and independent media, and ensure the safety of journalists and their ability to work without intimidation or harassment.

C. CPI, 2018 and India: India improved its ranking on CPI by 3 points, i.e. moving up from the earlier 81st position to 78th position. China ranked 87 and Pakistan ranked 117 (Table 13.1). Clearly, India is very low on the corruption perception index and remedial measures are needed to improve the situation.

Table 13.1: Corruption Perception Index (CPI) Rankings, 2018 Top 10 Countries plus India, China and Pakistan

Rank	Country	Score (out of 100)
1.	Denmark	88
2.	New Zealand	87
3.	Finland	85
4.	Singapore	85
5.	Sweden	85
6.	Switzerland	85
7.	Norway	84
8.	Netherlands	82
9.	Canada	81
10.	Luxembourg	81
78.	**India**	**41**
87.	China	39
117.	Pakistan	33

Source: Transparency International, *Corruption Perception Index, 2018*.

A number of initiatives need to be urgently pursued to rid the system of corruption, which is both morally abhorrent and imposes economic costs. Several legislative measures are needed. These include the establishment of an effective Lokpal, introduction of a law on public procurement and transparency, and the creation of a legislative framework governing the functioning of regulatory institutions so as to ensure both functional autonomy and accountability.

To combat corruption, it is imperative to ensure speedy prosecution and trial in corruption cases. The long delays in the judicial process are an important factor behind the growing cynicism about the rule of law in our system. Reforms in the legal process need to be put in place without further delays.

Endnote

1. Fiscal deficit, an internationally used concept, shows the excess of all expenditure, both revenue and capital, *over* revenue receipts plus non-debt capital receipts.
   Fiscal deficit = Total expenditure – (Revenue receipts + Non-debt capital receipts).
   Fiscal deficit is reflective of the total borrowing requirements of the Government. It measures the entire shortfall in the non-debt resources for financing the Central Government expenditure and fully reflects the impact of fiscal operations on the indebtedness of the Government by quantifying the total borrowings by the Government. It indicates the total borrowing requirements of the Government from all sources. These borrowings are from: (a) the public under various small saving schemes, (b) commercial banks, and other financial institutions, mainly through statutory liquidity ratio (SLR) instrument, and (c) the Reserve Bank of India. Fiscal deficit makes no distinction between different types of borrowings although the implication of borrowings from the Reserve Bank of India is different compared to borrowings from other sources.
   Fiscal deficit is met by borrowings which lead to internal debt of the Government. The servicing of this debt has become a serious problem. Public debt in India is mostly subscribed to by commercial banks and financial institutions. A judicious macro-management of the economy requires progressive reduction in the fiscal deficit and revenue deficit of the Government. With the discontinuance of the concept of overall deficit, fiscal deficit is now the key indicator of deficit. Any abnormal growth in fiscal deficit becomes a cause for worry for policy makers.

14

Challenges Ahead

The process of opening up of the Indian economy has given birth to a host of new challenges and opportunities. The spirit of the liberalisation process entails a conscious effort on the part of the policy makers to optimise on these opportunities-challenges trade-offs. The greatest challenge facing the Indian economy is to enhance its productivity and competitiveness so as to achieve a sustained growth in exports of goods and services. Growth prospects can be enhanced considerably by tapping the opportunities offered by the international economy in terms of markets, investment and technologies along with improvement in efficiency and absorbing excess capacity available in the economy.

14.1 Integration of Indian Economy with Global Economy

India's integration into the world economy since the initiation of economic reforms in 1991 has been remarkably rapid. Integration into the world economy implies more than just exports. In fact, India's financial integration with the world is deeper than before.

The access of Indian corporate sector to external funding has markedly increased in recent years. While funds are available domestically, foreign funding is perceived to be less expensive than domestic financing. On the promise of India's growth potential, foreign investors and lenders are willing to take risks and finance investment in India. These capital flows evidence the importance of external financing to the corporates and the depth of India's financial integration.

The Indian economy is now a relatively open economy with full current account convertibility and partial capital account convertibility. Developments in international markets are bound to affect the Indian economy and policy makers have to be vigilant in order to minimize the impact of adverse international developments on the domestic economy. India's vulnerability to global events is clearly marked.

While encouraging foreign investment flows, especially direct investment inflows, Government has adopted a more cautious approach in regard to debt flows. Debt flows in the form of external commercial borrowings are subject to ceilings and some end-use restrictions, which are modulated from time-to-time taking into account evolving macroeconomic and monetary conditions. Similarly, portfolio investment in government securities and corporate bonds are also subject to macro ceilings, which are also modulated from time-to-time. Prudential policies have attempted to prevent excessive recourse to foreign borrowings and dollarisation of the economy.

In regard to capital outflows, the policy framework has been progressively liberalised to enable the non-financial corporate sector to invest abroad and to acquire companies in the overseas market. Resident individuals are also permitted outflows subject to reasonable limits.

In short, Indian economy cannot remain insulated from global economic trends. Ever since the initiation of economic reforms in 1991, India is more integrated with the world economy than ever before. However, this integration has taken place gradually and with abundant precautions.

14.2 Rejection of Decoupling Hypothesis

Prior to the initiation of globalisation process in the 1990s and the establishment of WTO in 1995, countries around the world, particularly emerging market economies, enjoyed considerable leverage to shape their own national policies and policy-making mechanisms.

The decoupling hypothesis held that even if advanced economies went into a downturn, emerging economies will remain unscathed because of their substantial foreign exchange reserves, improved policy framework, robust corporate balance sheets and relatively healthy banking sector. In a rapidly globalizing world, the decoupling hypothesis was never totally persuasive.

With globalization and anti-protection rules of WTO, domestic economic policies of countries have increasingly come under the influence of international agencies and processes or by big private corporations and economic/financial players. This has led to the narrowed ability of governments and people to make choices from options in economic and even social policies.

14.2.1 U.S. Sub-prime Crisis: Decoupling hypothesis stood completely invalidated after the sub-prime crisis that emerged in the U.S. housing mortgage market in the second half of 2007, and snowballed into a global financial and economic crisis. What started off as a sub-prime crisis turned successively into a global banking crisis, global financial crisis and then a global economic crisis (recession). It was billed by experts as the worst since the Great Depression of late 1920s and early 1930s that originated in the advanced economies and rapidly engulfed the whole world.

The financial turmoil which surfaced in August 2007 in the U.S. financial system as a result of defaults of sub-prime mortgage loans blew into an unprecedented financial crisis engulfing international money, credit, equity and foreign exchange markets. It was preceded by an extended phase of buoyant world economy characterized by output expansion, burgeoning world trade, favourable financial and economic conditions, liquidity overhang and low interest rates. Economists termed it as a period of Great Moderation.

With the start of sub-prime crisis, the global financial landscape changed significantly during the course of 2008-09 wherein several large international financial institutions either failed or were restructured, with the support of very large government interventions in many countries, to prevent imminent collapse. The significant deterioration in global financial conditions since mid-September 2008, led to severe disruptions in the short-term funding markets, widening of risk spreads, sharp fall in equity prices and inactivity in the markets for asset-backed securities.

Resultantly, the strain on the balance sheets of financial institutions increased, threatening the viability of some of the most well-known financial entities in the world. The freezing up of credit markets necessitated extraordinary actions on the part of central banks and governments in countries across the world to mitigate the risks posed by the financial crisis.

Even though institutions in most of the emerging economies did not have direct exposure to the toxic assets, these economies suffered the consequences of the economic recession, caused by U.S. sub-prime crisis in 2007.

In a rapidly globalising world, the decoupling theory has not stood the test of time. U.S. sub-prime crisis reinforced the notion that in a globalized world no country can be an island.

14.3 Global Economic Crises Are Contagious

Economic malaises are contagious. A crisis in developed countries is bound to have an impact around the world. Monetary policy developments in the leading economies not only affect developing countries domestically, but also have a profound impact on the rest of the world through changes in risk premia and search for yield, leading to significant switches in capital flows. Changes in the monetary policy in the U.S. are dictated by internal compulsions—to maintain employment and price stability—but the consequent volatility in capital flows impinges on exchange rate movements and more generally on asset and commodity prices. The monetary policy dynamics of the advanced economies thus involve sharp adjustments for the developing countries.

Private capital flows to developing countries have grown rapidly since the 1980s, but with increased volatility over time. Large capital flows to the developing countries can be attributed to a variety of push and pull factors. The pull factors that have led to higher capital flows in these countries have included the following: (a) strong growth over the past decade, (b) reduction in inflation, (c) macroeconomic stability, (d) opening up of capital accounts and (e) buoyant growth prospects.

The major push factor is the stance of monetary policy in the advanced economies. Periods of loose monetary policy coupled with search for yield in the advanced economies encourages large capital inflows to developing countries and vice versa in periods of tighter monetary policy. Thus, swings in monetary policy in the advanced economies lead to cycles and volatility in capital flows to developing countries. Innovations in information technology have also contributed to the two-way movement in capital flows. In response to these factors, capital flows to developing countries since the early 1980s have grown over time, but with large volatility.

The transmission of economic crises in the developed world to emerging economies takes place *via* both trade and financial channels. In short, modern day world economies sink and swim together.

14.3.1 Contagious Nature of Business Cycles: Forces of globalisation have led to substantial increases in international trade as well as financial flows since early 1990s. An issue in this context is whether increased integration has led to a larger degree of synchronisation of business cycles across countries. A global shock—say, an increase in global crude oil prices—will affect all countries simultaneously.

For countries quite open to external trade, economic developments in their partner countries can get transmitted through exports and imports and this is expected to increase the co-movement of output across countries. A diversified structure of export destinations tends to weaken the co-movement of business cycles.

Trade as well as financial integration allows countries to specialise in industries in which they have a comparative advantage. This can result in more vulnerability to industry- or country-specific shocks but reduce cross-country output movements.

14.4 The China Factor

Despite the euphoria surrounding India's rapid development, many are starting to question just how well the emergent power can compete against much larger and much more developed neighbouring rival China. In one sense, India's rise has been overshadowed by what has been happening in China over the past four decades. On a more positive note, China's rise has provided an example to India as to what to emulate and what to avoid. In fact, in recent years India's growth has mirrored that of China.

However, current Chinese slowdown has important implications for India. Chinese excess capacity in commodity-related sectors such as steel and aluminium will lead to a surge in imports into India. India should strengthen procedures that allow WTO-consistent and hence legitimate actions against dumping.

14.5 India's Falling Competitiveness Ranking

The objective of competition is met by ensuring that there are sufficient numbers of producers so that no producer can attain a position of dominance. If the nature of the industry is such that dominance in terms of market share cannot be avoided, it seeks to ensure that there is no abuse on account of this dominance. Competition policy also seeks to forestall other forms of market failure, such as formation of cartels, leading to collusive pricing, division of markets and joint decisions to reduce supply. Mergers and acquisitions also need to be regulated as they reduce competition.

The aim of the competition policy is to create a framework of policies and regulations that will inform other policies to facilitate competitive outcomes in the market. Competition policy is a critical component of any overall economic policy framework. Competition policy is intended to promote efficiency and to maximize consumer/social welfare. It also promotes creation of a business environment, which improves static and dynamic efficiencies, leads to efficient resource allocation and consumer welfare, and in which abuse of market power is prevented/curbed. It also promotes good governance by restricting rent seeking practices of economic actors.

14.5.1 India's Rank in Global Competitiveness Index: Since 1979, Global Competitiveness Index (GCI) has been released annually by the World Economic Forum based in Geneva (Switzerland).

GCI is designed to help policy-makers, business leaders and other stakeholders around the world to shape their economic strategies in the era of globalization.

The competitiveness index integrates aspects that drive productivity and growth. It emphasizes the role of human capital, innovation, resilience and agility, as not only drivers but also defining features of economic success. It calls for better use of technology for economic leapfrogging—but also cautions that this is only possible as part of a holistic approach with other factors of competitiveness. Finally, it offers objective, data-driven analysis for dispassionate, future-oriented, and rational policy-making.

GCI ranks competitiveness of various countries through 103 indicators under the following 12 parameters:

1. Market size.
2. Macroeconomic stability.
3. Financial system.
4. Infrastructure.
5. Health.
6. Business dynamism.
7. Institutions.
8. Labour market.
9. Innovation capability.
10. Skills.
11. Product market.
12. ICT adoption.

According to GCI Report released in October 2019, India

ranked at 68th place in a survey of 141 countries of the world. India ranked at 58th position and 63rd position in the 2018 and 2017 Reports respectively. The country slipped 10 notches in the last one year and 5 notches in the last two years.

In the 2019 Report, India ranked high in terms of macroeconomic stability (particularly inflation management) and market size. It also found India's financial sector as relatively deep and stable. However, 2019 Report pointed out major shortcomings in some of the basic enablers of competitiveness. Thus, India faired poorly in terms of security and incidence of terrorism. Notably, India lost ground in the ranking despite a relatively stable score (Table 14.1). It indicated faster improvements of several countries previously ranked lower. Rankings of top 10 countries along with China, India and Pakistan are shown in Table 14.1. Singapore is the most competitive economy of the world followed by US and Hong Kong.

Table 14.1: Rankings of Top Ten Countries plus China, India and Pakistan in Global Competitiveness Index for 2019

Rank	Country	Score (scale ranges from 0 to 100)
1 (2)	Singapore	84.8 (83.5)
2 (1)	USA	83.7 (85.6)
3 (7)	Hong Kong	83.1 (82.3)
4 (6)	Netherlands	82.4 (82.4)
5 (4)	Switzerland	82.3 (82.6)
6 (5)	Japan	82.3 (82.5)
7 (3)	Germany	81.8 (82.8)
8 (9)	Sweden	81.2 (81.7)
9 (8)	UK	81.2 (82.0)
10 (10)	Denmark	81.2 (80.6)
28 (28)	**China**	**73.9 (72.6)**
68 (58)	**India**	**61.4 (62.0)**
110 (107)	**Pakistan**	**51.4 (51.1)**

Figures in parentheses indicate rank and scores of the country in 2018.
Source: World Economic Forum, *Global Competitiveness Report 2019*.

The concept and the role of competition are relatively new to the Indian business community. There is, therefore, a pressing need to increase the level of awareness about the benefits of competition and the contribution of the competition law in this respect among the public, more particularly among the business community.

India can fully realise its potential only if it continues to pursue growth-friendly economic policies. India's growth prospects critically hinge on prudent fiscal stance, extending its openness to foreign trade and investment, increased investment in transport and energy infrastructure and improved health and educational standards. Furthermore, farm productivity must rise to sustain high growth and inflation must remain under control.

To sum up, India is home to 130 crore people, of whom 90 crore are of working age. These 90 crore need jobs to sustain themselves and India's growth. These jobs can only be provided by the sustained growth of the manufacturing and service sectors in India.

India's citizens have higher expectations about their future today, than they have ever had before. They have seen the economy grow much faster in recent years than it did earlier, and deliver visible benefits to a large number of people. This has understandably raised the expectations of all sections, especially those who have benefited less. People are now much more aware of what is possible, and they will settle for no less.

Growth must make a demonstrable difference to the lives of the poorest and most vulnerable citizens. India has the potential and the means to secure a reasonable standard of living for all of its citizens. Inclusive growth necessarily implies concerted effort, by all levels of government, to invest in the delivery of public services, particularly those which promote progress in social sectors like health and education. However, to achieve this potential, it is necessary that resources are mobilised and deployed in such a manner that the benefits of growth percolate to ordinary people, particularly those living below poverty line.

The socio-economically disadvantaged are yet to benefit from economic reforms. The challenge to overcome the scourge of poverty remains a daunting task. The support of the poor for reforms and their involvement in the development process can be achieved only if they start benefiting from the liberal economic policies of the Central and State Governments. Economic reforms must be guided by compassion and distributive justice.

India's growth story is all well but its moral virtues—in terms of equity and environment—are falling by the wayside. The message is clear: The growth process must be made as inclusive and as environment-friendly as possible.

The challenge ahead, therefore, is to create the jobs to employ India's rapidly growing youth base, and the only means of doing so is to catalyze increased private investment in India. Today's investment equals tomorrow's jobs, and so the Government of India has embarked on the ambitious Make-in-India initiative to create jobs.

The growth of business in India requires concerted action on several fronts—infrastructure, capital markets, trade facilitation and skills—but the stark reality is that India remains a difficult place to do business. A disproportionately high regulatory burden is borne by businesses in India today. A majority of the regulatory burden imposed on business is due to the plethora of laws, rules, regulations and procedures enforced by governments at different levels. This gives rise to a wide number of registrations, licenses and no objection certificates that businesses must obtain.

It is encouraging to note that the Government of India has embarked on ambitious reforms focused on starting a business, resolving insolvency, enforcing contracts, and trading across borders. Aatmanirbhar Bharat Abhiyan (Self-reliant India Initiative) announced by Prime Minister Narendra Modi on May 12, 2020 is a step in the right direction.

15

Economic Impact of Lockdowns

Pre-COVID, India's growth story was largely positive on the strength of domestic absorption, and the economy was registering a steady pace of economic growth. Moreover, its other macroeconomic parameters like inflation, fiscal deficit and current account balance had exhibited distinct signs of improvement. International Monetary Fund (IMF) had praised India for implementing important reforms including introduction of goods and services tax (GST), inflation targeting and Insolvency and Bankruptcy Code. In short, Indian economy was ready to shift gears to the next level to achieve accelerated growth.

15.1 COVID-19 and Lockdowns

With all the above favourable factors for high growth rate in place, the outbreak of coronavirus epidemic in China was reported. On March 11, 2020, the World Health Organization (WHO) declared the epidemic as a pandemic. Normal economic activities around the world were disrupted. Lockdowns were declared in most of the countries for varying periods to cope with the medical crisis. Global economy was badly shattered and continues to remain in turmoil. There is tremendous loss of production, income and employment. This crisis is yet to come full circle.

On June 8, 2020, the World Bank released a report titled *Global Economic Prospects* and predicted that world economy would shrink by 5.2 percent in 2020. Advanced economies would experience growth falling by 7 percent while emerging economies (including India) as a group would see a growth decline of 2.5 percent. According to the report, Indian economy would shrink by 3.2 percent in the fiscal year 2020-21. The report, which contained an assessment of economic shocks from the coronavirus pandemic shutdowns, noted that the pandemic had plunged the world into a severe recession, deepest since the Second World War.

On March 24, 2020 Prime Minister Narendra Modi, in a televised address to the nation, announced a stringent countrywide lockdown from March 25 to April 14 which was extended from time-to-time until June 30 but with gradual relaxations. The extended lockdown, now being reversed, to slow down the spread of the disease, is expected to adversely affect the growth rate of the Indian economy during 2020-21 and beyond. There are fears that the economy may actually shrink.

15.2 Fall in Government Revenues

At the start of the nationwide lockdown, all transport (railways, airways, metros, road transport) was halted. Business establishments were closed down. The supply of essential goods and services only was allowed. The severity of the lockdown can be gauged from the fact that not a single motor vehicle was sold in the country during the month of April 2020. Gross GST collections which totalled ₹ 1,05,366 crore in the month of February fell to ₹ 97,597 crore in March and further down to ₹ 43,000 crore in April 2020. The country is going through an unprecedented crisis owing to COVID pandemic.

It was in January 2018 in Davos (Switzerland) that Prime Minister Narendra Modi first expressed his ambition to make India a 5 trillion dollar economy by 2024-25. He reiterated the target at the Governing Council Meeting of NITI Aayog in New Delhi in June 2019.

To achieve the objective of becoming a US$ 5 trillion economy by 2024-25, *Economic Survey, 2018-19* assumed an average real annual growth rate in GDP of 8 percent from 2020-21 to 2024-25. It also assumed an inflation rate of 4 percent. This implied a nominal growth rate of 12 percent.

As things stand, it is difficult, if not impossible, to realize the 5 trillion dollar dream.

But these dark clouds have a silver lining. In spite of massive economic loss due to lockdown, India can look forward to revival of the economy in the near future. Compared to other developing economies, India has several strengths that can help mitigate the adverse effects of COVID-induced slowdown. The Government has taken several measures in this direction and the economy is expected to return to a high growth trajectory. As the monetary and fiscal stimuli work their way through, and calm and confidence are restored in the global markets, India can see an economic turnaround soon.

This belief that Indian economy will rebound lies in its resilience shown in recent years. For example, the economy escaped almost unscathed during the unprecedented financial crisis of 2007-08 when economies of developed countries went topsy-turvy. Financial giants, including Lehman Brothers, collapsed like a house of cards.

15.3 Lockdowns and Agricultural Sector

While the countrywide lockdown brought most economic activities to a grinding halt in urban areas, rural India continued to be normal in view of exemptions from restrictions allowed to farmers to conduct farming operations, including harvesting and transporting their produce to grain markets. These exemptions helped to maintain continuity in supply chain, especially in view of the harvesting and sowing season. Food Corporation of India and State Governments carried out massive procurement of *rabi* crops, mainly wheat.

Not only cultivation, but agriculture-related activities—plantation, horticulture, cattle breeding, fishing, poultry farming, dairy farming—have also remained, by and large, immune to the Covid crisis and their future growth is assured.

India's foodgrains production was 285 million tonnes (MT) in 2018-19 which rose to a record level of 295 MT in 2019-20. The target for 2020-21 has been set at 299 MT.

On April 15, 2020, India Meteorological Department (IMD) predicted normal rainfall over India during the South-West monsoon season (June to September), with an error margin of ± 5 percent. Based on this, it has been estimated that India will harvest a record output of 299 million tonnes of foodgrains during the 2020-21 agricultural season. A vibrant agricultural sector is a guarantee for meeting the primary needs of the poor.

15.4 Low Crude Oil Prices

The petroleum sector dominates India's current energy use. This is one of the most vulnerable sectors in the Indian energy scenario. As an oil deficit country, India is dependent on imports of crude oil to the extent of 85 percent of its total requirements. India is the third biggest importer of crude oil after China and Japan.

Crude oil ruled at US$ 147 per barrel (highest in history) in August 2009. At the beginning of 2020, global oil market was experiencing high oil output as a result of production increases in US, Canada, Russia and OPEC (Organization for Petroleum Exporting Countries) countries. With Covid outbreak in China, and the lockdown of Wuhan, a major industrial hub, oil prices tumbled down from US$ 68 per barrel in early January 2020 to US$ 53 per barrel in early February.

As the Covid outbreak grew into a pandemic, countries around the world were affected, causing panic and unplanned lockouts. Industries were shut down and transport and travel activities came to a screeching halt. This led to fall in oil prices and price wars (in the form of discounts) among major oil exporters. Oil prices dipped as low as US$ 20 per barrel, causing immense harm to oil-dependent countries of West Asia. After recovery, in the wake of easing of lockdowns, oil prices are hovering around US$ 40 per barrel.

Covid-related crash in crude oil prices has proved to be a windfall for India. Import bill has reduced, making the current account deficit in the balance of payments more manageable.

Economic Survey, 2017-18 (Government of India) had estimated that, "a US$ 10 per barrel increase in the price of oil reduces growth by 0.2-0.3 percentage points, increases WPI (wholesale price index) inflation by about 1.7 percentage points and worsens the CAD (current account deficit) by about US$ 9-10 billion dollars". If these calculations are applied in the reverse, one can imagine the enormous benefit which India is enjoying as a result of current low prices of crude oil.

15.5 China's Loss Can be India's Gain

The current world hostility towards China, the epicentre of coronavirus, can be converted into opportunity for India. Post-Covid, US-China trade war is likely to accelerate. On April 29, 2020, President Trump hinted at the possibility of US claiming damages from China for latter's mishandling of the coronavirus outbreak. It is claimed that the coronavirus originated in a laboratory in Wuhan and China failed to stop it at the source. The developed world, led by Australia, is demanding an international probe into the causes of the virus spread, which China is vehemently trying to stonewall.

In such a scenario, economic and financial distancing from China may be a policy prescription not only for US and its Western allies, but also for other countries including India. US and Western companies, at the behest of their governments, are planning to shift their manufacturing units and withdraw investment from China. The pandemic has led several companies towards a realisation that de-coupling their supply chains from China may be necessary to mitigate risk arising out of natural and geopolitical disturbances.

Moreover, rising US-China tensions on South China Sea (SCS) are scaring away global corporate giants, particularly US-based, from that potentially troubled and contentious region. On July 13, 2020, US Secretary of State Mike Pompeo in a statement rejected all of China's maritime claims in the SCS as completely unlawful. It is noteworthy that in 2016 an Order of the Arbitral Tribunal, constituted under the 1982 Law of the Sea, had rejected China's maritime claims in SCS. US seems to be aligning its SCS policy with this Order which experts believe is a major shift and bound to anger China.

Owing to reasons stated above, transnational companies and other big firms are turning away from China and looking at India as the next best location for their business activities.

We can be their next best destination provided we ready ourselves to leverage this opportunity. This requires government incentives, Centre-State co-ordination, and joint venture offers from Indian corporates. Although India has jumped on the ease-of-doing-business rank in recent years, it is yet to break into the top 50 countries.

In the recent past, most companies which withdrew from China preferred Taiwan, Thailand and Vietnam for re-location. Very few opted for India. It underscores the need to make India more business-friendly for prospective foreign investors.

For example, India can be an attractive hub for drugs at a time when China faces hostility, distrust and quality issues. Presently, China controls 55 percent of API, a key raw material for drug manufacturers, market in the world. On March 21, 2020, the Union Cabinet approved a ₹ 10,000 crore incentive-based scheme to promote domestic manufacturing of APIs by setting up bulk drug parks. India can also leverage the current anti-China feelings to push its exports globally in markets likely to be vacated by China.

15.6 India as Preferred Destination for Foreign Investment

Of late, India has become an attractive destination for foreign investment owing, among other factors, to its large and rapidly growing consumer market, a developed commercial banking network, availability of skilled manpower and a package of fiscal incentives for foreign investors. The top investing countries in India include Mauritius, US, Japan, UK and Netherlands. The most important sectors attracting foreign investment are electrical equipment including computer software, transportation industry, telecommunications, and fuels.

India continues to retain its position as a preferred destination for investments. In her speech to the Parliament while presenting the Budget for 2019-20 (Final) on July 5, 2019, Finance Minister

Nirmala Sitharaman remarked, "FDI inflows into India have remained robust despite global headwinds. Global foreign direct investment (FDI) flows slid by 13 percent in 2018, to US$ 1.3 trillion from US$ 1.5 trillion the previous year—the third consecutive annual decline, according to UNCTAD's World Investment Report 2019. India's FDI inflows in 2018-19 remained strong at US$ 64.375 billion marking a 6 percent growth over the previous year".

This pick-up indicates improvement in confidence of foreign investors in the Indian economy which offers a large and rapidly growing consumer market and where English is the preferred language of business.

The Public Investment Fund of Saudi Arabia announced on June 18, 2020 that it would invest US$ 1.5 billion (₹ 11,367 crore) in Jio platforms for a 2.32 percent stake in the top Indian telecom operator. Similarly, Google announced on July 13, 2020 that it would invest nearly US$ 10 billion (₹ 75,000 crore) into developing digital infrastructure and for funding innovations in India over the next five to seven years. Google would help to expand the scope of digital payments using Google Pay, and develop low-cost smartphones and other products and services. This indicated how major US-based companies, after turning away from China, are looking at India. It is also a reflection of foreign investors' confidence in the future of India and its digital economy.

15.7 Diversified Industrial and Infrastructural Base of India

India is a highly diversified and self-sufficient economy. This is in sharp contrast to single-commodity (crude oil) economies of West Asia where almost all goods and services are imported except oil.

India has established a strong and diversified manufacturing base for the production of a wide variety of basic and capital goods to meet the requirements of various sectors including heavy electricals, power generation and transmission, process equipment, automobiles, ships, mining, chemicals, and crude oil refining. There is a considerable potential for growth which, in a globalized world economy, has to be based on improving productivity and competitiveness. Innovation and adoption of new technologies are the key factors in competitiveness. In the Indian context, opening of the economy and the subsequent entry of international players has substantially enhanced the need for production of goods and services matching international standards.

India has systematically rolled out a public-private-partnership (PPP) programme for the delivery of high-priority public utilities and infrastructure and developed what is perhaps one of the largest PPP programmes in the world. Government is promoting PPP as an effective tool for bringing private sector efficiencies in the creation of economic and social infrastructure assets and for delivery of quality public services. Traditionally, infrastructure development was engineered through the public sector. However, in the face of scarcity of public resources and the need to shift these into health and education, efforts have been made to induct private participation in the development of infrastructure. These efforts have met with a fair degree of success.

Appendix

Reforms Introduced in India as per Doing Business Reports of World Bank: 2008 to 2020

According to *Doing Business Report* of the World Bank for various years, following reforms were introduced in India from time-to-time to enhance business activities.

Doing Business Report	Reforms introduced
2008	**Getting Credit:** India strengthened its secured transactions system by launching a unified and geographically centralized collateral registry and started to provide credit information on firms at the private credit bureau. **Trading across Borders:** India made trading across borders easier by introducing ICEGATE—an electronic data interchange system making it possible to lodge customs declarations through the internet and facilitating the operation of a risk management system, an electronic payment system and an electronic manifest system that allows shipping lines to submit their cargo manifest in advance.
2009	**Trading across Borders:** India reduced the time for exporting by implementing an electronic data interchange system.
2010	**Resolving Insolvency:** India made resolving insolvency easier by increasing the effectiveness of processes and thereby reducing the time required.
2011	**Starting a Business:** India eased business start-up by establishing an online VAT registration system and

	replacing the physical stamp previously required with an online version. **Paying Taxes:** India reduced the administrative burden of paying taxes by abolishing the fringe benefit tax and improving electronic payment.
2012	**Paying Taxes:** India eased the administrative burden of paying taxes for firms by introducing mandatory electronic ling and payment for value added tax.
2013	**Dealing with Construction Permits:** India reduced the time required to obtain a building permit by establishing strict time limits for pre-construction approvals.
2015	**Starting a Business:** India made starting a business easier by considerably reducing the registration fees, but also made it more difficult by introducing a requirement to file a declaration before the commencement of business operations. These changes apply to both Delhi and Mumbai. **Getting Electricity:** In India the utility in Mumbai made getting electricity less costly by reducing the security deposit for a new connection. **Protecting Minority Investors:** India strengthened minority investor protections by requiring greater disclosure of conflicts of interest by board members, increasing the remedies available in case of prejudicial related-party transactions and introducing additional safeguards for shareholders of privately-held companies. This reform applies to both Delhi and Mumbai.
2016	**Starting a Business:** India made starting a business easier by eliminating the minimum capital requirement and the need to obtain a certificate to commence business operations. This reform applies to both Delhi and Mumbai. **Getting Electricity:** The utility in Delhi made the process for getting an electricity connection simpler and faster by eliminating the internal wiring inspection by the Electrical Inspectorate. The utility in Mumbai reduced

	the procedures and time required to connect to electricity by improving internal work processes and coordination.
2017	**Getting Electricity:** India made getting electricity faster and cheaper by streamlining the process of getting a new commercial electricity connection. This reform impacts Delhi. **Paying Taxes:** India made paying taxes easier by introducing an electronic system for paying employee state insurance contributions. This reform applies to both Mumbai and Delhi. **Trading across Borders:** India made exporting and importing easier by launching Customs Electronic Commerce Interchange Gateway portal and simplifying border and documentary compliance procedures. This reform applies to both New Delhi and Mumbai. **Enforcing Contracts:** India made enforcing contracts easier by creating dedicated divisions to resolve commercial cases. This reform applies to both Mumbai and Delhi.
2018	**Starting a Business:** India made starting a business faster by merging the applications for the permanent account number (PAN) and the tax account number (TAN) and by improving the online application system. Mumbai also made starting a business faster by merging the applications for value added tax and the profession tax (PT). **Dealing with Construction Permits:** India reduced the number of procedures and time required to obtain a building permit by implementing an online system that has streamlined the process at the Municipality of New Delhi and Municipality of Greater Mumbai. **Getting Credit:** India strengthened access to credit by amending the rules on priority of secured creditors outside reorganization proceedings and by adopting a new law on insolvency that provides a time limit and clear grounds for relief to the automatic stay for secured creditors during reorganization procedures. This reform impacts the data for both Mumbai and Delhi.

	Protecting Minority Investors: Protections for minority investors were strengthened by increasing the remedies available in cases of prejudicial transactions between interested parties. This reform applies to both Delhi and Mumbai. **Paying Taxes:** In both Delhi and Mumbai, paying taxes was made easier by requiring payments to the Employees Provident Fund to be made electronically, and introducing administrative measures that make it easier to comply with corporate income tax regulations. **Trading Across Borders:** In Mumbai, reducing the time taken to comply with import regulations at Nhava Sheva port made it much quicker to trade across borders. In Delhi and Mumbai, the elimination of merchant overtime fees and the increased use of electronic and mobile platforms reduced the time taken to comply with both export and import regulations. **Enforcing Contracts:** In both Delhi and Mumbai, the introduction of the National Judicial Data Grid made it possible to generate case management reports on local courts, thereby making it easier to enforce contracts. **Resolving Insolvency:** India made resolving insolvency easier by adopting a new insolvency and bankruptcy code that introduced a reorganization procedure for corporate debtors and facilitated continuation of the debtor's business during insolvency proceedings. This reform applies to both Delhi and Mumbai.
2019	**Starting a Business:** India made starting a business easier by fully integrating multiple application forms into a general incorporation form. India also replaced the value added tax with the GST (Goods and Services Tax) for which the registration process is faster. These reforms apply to both Delhi and Mumbai. At the same time, Mumbai abolished the practice of site inspections for registering companies under the Shops and Establishments Act. **Dealing with Construction Permits:** India streamlined the process of obtaining a building permit and made it faster and less expensive to obtain a construction permit. It also improved building quality control by introducing

	decennial liability and insurance. This reform applies to both Delhi and Mumbai. **Getting Electricity:** The Delhi Electricity Regulatory Commission reduced charges for low voltage connections. Getting electricity was also made easier in Delhi through a reduction in the time for the utility to carry out the external connection works. **Getting Credit:** India strengthened access to credit by amending its insolvency law. Secured creditors are now given absolute priority over other claims within insolvency proceedings. This reform applies to both Delhi and Mumbai. **Paying Taxes:** India made paying taxes easier by replacing many indirect taxes with a single indirect tax, the GST, for the entire country. India also made paying taxes less costly by reducing the corporate income tax rate and the employees' provident funds scheme rate paid by the employer. This reform applies to both Delhi and Mumbai. **Trading across Borders:** India reduced the time and cost to export and import through various initiatives, including the implementation of electronic sealing of containers, the upgrading of port infrastructure and allowing electronic submission of supporting documents with digital signatures. This reform applies to both Delhi and Mumbai. **Labour Market Regulation:** India (Mumbai) changed regulations pertaining to weekly holiday work, overtime hours and paid annual leave.
2020	**Starting a Business:** India made starting a business easier by abolishing filing fees for the SPICe company incorporation form, electronic memorandum of association, and articles of association. **Dealing with Construction Permits:** India streamlined the process, reduced the time and cost of obtaining construction permits, and improved building quality control by strengthening professional certification requirements. **Trading Across Borders**: India made trading across borders easier by enabling post-clearance audits,

	integrating trade stakeholders in a single electronic platform, upgrading port infrastructures, and enhancing the electronic submission of documents. **Resolving Insolvency**: India made resolving insolvency easier by promoting reorganization proceedings in practice.

Bibliography

Bloomberg (New York), Bloomberg Innovation Index, 2019.

Concern Worldwide and Welt Hunger Hilfe, *Global Hunger Index, 2019.*

Economist Intelligence Unit, *Government E-payments Adoption Ranking Report, September 2018.*

Government of India, Ministry of Finance, *Economic Survey* (various issues).

—Ministry of Finance, *Budget Papers* (various years).

—Ministry of Agriculture and Farmers Welfare, *Annual Report* (various years).

—Ministry of Law, Justice, and Company Affairs, *Constitution of India.*

—Ministry of Micro, Small and Medium Enterprises, *Annual Report, 2018-19.*

IMD World Competitiveness Centre, *World Digital Competitiveness Ranking, 2019.*

NITI Aayog, *India: Three Year Action Agenda (2017-18 to 2019-20)*, August 2017.

—*Strategy for New India @75*, November 2018.

—*India Innovation Index, 2019.*

Reserve Bank of India, *Report on Currency and Finance* (various years).

—*Report of the High-Level Committee on Deepening of Digital Payments* (Chairman: Nandan Nilekani), May 2019.

Transparency International, *Corruption Perception Index, 2018.*

United Nations, World Intellectual Property Organization (WIPO), *Global Innovation Index 2019.*

World Bank, *Doing Business Report* (various years).

—*Trade Logistics in the Global Economy* (various years).

—*Global Economic Prospects, 2020*

World Economic Forum, *The Global Competitiveness Report 2019.*

—*Travel and Tourism Competitiveness Report 2019.*

Websites

Ministry of Finance, Government of India

Ministry of Agriculture and Farmers Welfare

Ministry of Commerce and Industry
Ministry of Rural Development
Ministry of Micro, Small and Medium Enterprises
Ministry of Skill Development and Entrepreneurship
Reserve Bank of India
Securities and Exchange Board of India (SEBI)
NITI Aayog

Index